Better Homes and Gardens®

Steaks, Ribs, Chops

and all the fixin's that make 'em great

Better Homes and Gardens® Books

Des Moines, Iowa

Better Homes and Gardens® Books
An imprint of Meredith® Books

Steaks, Ribs, Chops
and all the fixin's that make 'em great
Editor: Kristi M. Fuller
Recipe Development: Marcia Kay Stanley, Susan Parenti
Contributing Writer: John DeMers
Designer: Matt Strelecki
Copy Chief: Catherine Hamrick
Copy and Production Editor: Terri Fredrickson
Contributing Proofreaders: Sheila Mauck, Debra Morris Smith
Photography: Jim Krantz, Peter Krumhardt
Photograph on page 32: Will Van Overbeek
Cover Illustrations: Michael Halbert
Electronic Production Coordinator: Paula Forest
Editorial and Design Assistants: Judy Bailey, Karen Schirm
Test Kitchen Director: Sharon Stilwell
Test Kitchen Product Supervisor: Marilyn Cornelius
Food Stylists: Janet Pittman, Jill Hoefler
Production Director: Douglas M. Johnston
Production Manager: Pam Kvitne
Assistant Prepress Manager: Margie J. Schenkelberg

Meredith® Books
Editor in Chief: James D. Blume
Design Director: Matt Strelecki
Managing Editor: Gregory H. Kayko
Executive Food Editor: Lisa Holderness

Director, Sales & Marketing, Retail: Michael A. Peterson
Director, Sales & Marketing, Special Markets: Rita McMullen
Director, Sales & Marketing, Home & Garden Center Channel:
    Ray Wolf
Director, Operations: George A. Susral

Vice President, General Manager: Jamie L. Martin

***Better Homes and Gardens*® Magazine**
Editor in Chief: Jean LemMon
Executive Food Editor: Nancy Byal

Meredith Publishing Group
President, Publishing Group: Christopher M. Little
Vice President, Consumer Marketing & Development: Hal Oringer

Meredith Corporation
Chairman and Chief Executive Officer: William T. Kerr

Chairman of the Executive Committee: E. T. Meredith III

All of us at Better Homes and Gardens® Books are dedicated to providing you with the information and ideas you need to create delicious foods. We welcome your comments and suggestions. Write to us at: Better Homes and Gardens® Books, Cookbook Editorial Department, 1716 Locust St., Des Moines, IA 50309-3023.

If you would like to order additional copies of any of our books, please check with your local bookstore.

Today's Menu

Steaks ⟶	**6**
Ribs ⟶	**32**
CHOPS ⟶	**54**
Smoked ⟶	**72**
fixin's ⟶	**88**
desserts ⟶	**100**

index ⟶ **116**   metric conversions ⟶ **120**

Time to Eat

Meat lovers, rejoice. This is *your* book. Steakhouses and BBQ joints have made a comeback, but you don't have to trek across the U.S. to find the choicest steaks, ribs, or chops from restaurant gurus. Top chefs from more than 15 popular restaurants across the country share their secret recipes in this special cookbook. Check out the chapter that features recipes just for your smoker. (No smoker? Directions for smoking on your grill are also included.) And, don't fret about what to serve on the side. Our side dish and dessert chapters make it easy. Just the aromas from this hearty, satisfying fare will round up your tired and hungry bunch. While you're at it, check out the scenery. It's bold, sassy, and one of a kind—like every tasty recipe.

Chapter 1

Steaks

Jalapeño-Glazed Ribeyes
with Corn Relish

Prep Time: 20 minutes
Grilling Time: 16 minutes

¼ cup jalapeño pepper jelly
¼ cup catsup
4 beef ribeye steaks, cut 1 inch thick
   (about 2½ pounds total)
2 tablespoons jalapeño pepper jelly
1 tablespoon lime juice
½ teaspoon chili powder
¼ teaspoon ground cumin
1 10-ounce package frozen whole
   kernel corn, thawed (2 cups)
¾ cup chopped red sweet pepper
¼ cup finely chopped green onions
1 fresh jalapeño pepper, seeded and
   finely chopped (optional)

For glaze, in a small bowl stir together the ¼ cup pepper jelly and the catsup. Set aside.

To grill indirectly, in a grill with a cover arrange preheated coals around a drip pan. Test for medium heat above pan. Place steaks on the grill rack directly over the drip pan. Cover and grill to desired doneness, brushing with the glaze the last 5 minutes of grilling time. (Allow 16 to 20 minutes for medium-rare doneness or 20 to 24 minutes for medium doneness.)

Meanwhile, for relish, in a saucepan stir together the 2 tablespoons pepper jelly, the lime juice, chili powder, and cumin. Cook and stir until jelly is melted and mixture is bubbly. Stir in corn, sweet pepper, onion, and the fresh jalapeño (if using). Cook and stir just until heated through. Season with salt. Serve steaks with the corn relish. Makes 4 servings.

To broil: Place steaks on the unheated rack of a broiler pan. Broil steaks 3 to 4 inches from the heat to desired doneness, turning the steaks once and brushing with the glaze during the last 5 minutes of broiling time. (Allow 10 to 12 minutes for medium-rare or 12 to 15 minutes for medium doneness.)

To grill directly: Grill the steaks on the grill rack of an uncovered grill directly over medium coals to desired doneness, turning steaks once and brushing with glaze the last 5 minutes of grilling time. (Allow 8 to 12 minutes for medium-rare doneness or 12 to 15 minutes for medium doneness.)

The flavors of the Southwest add sizzle to these steaks. Using jalapeño pepper jelly, whip up a quick spicy-sweet glaze that will impress your guests. The pepper jelly also adds a mild kick to the corn relish. But if you really like warmth, add a jalapeño pepper to the relish.

On the broad pampas of Argentina—even in bustling South American culture capitals such as Buenos Aires—everybody loves dinner at the *churrasco,* a cross between a barbecue joint and a steakhouse. At least one churrasco specialty is called *chimichurri,* a quick sauce or basting liquid based on Italian parsley and oregano. Try it for a final zap of flavor to an already grand piece of grilled beef.

Argentinean-Style Steak

Prep Time: 30 minutes
Grilling Time: 16 minutes

2   beef T-bone or porterhouse steaks,
       cut 1 inch thick
3   tablespoons olive oil
2   tablespoons snipped fresh Italian flat-leaf parsley
1   tablespoon snipped fresh oregano or 1 teaspoon dried
       oregano, crushed
2   to 3 cloves garlic, minced
¼   teaspoon salt
¼   teaspoon ground red pepper

In a grill with a cover arrange preheated coals around a drip pan. Test for medium heat above pan. Place steaks on grill rack directly over pan. Cover and grill steaks to desired doneness. (Allow 16 to 20 minutes for medium-rare doneness or 20 to 24 minutes for medium doneness.)

Meanwhile, for the sauce, stir together the olive oil, parsley, oregano, garlic, salt, and red pepper. Spoon the sauce on top of the steaks for the last 2 minutes of grilling. Makes 4 servings.

To grill directly: Grill the steaks on an uncovered grill directly over medium coals to desired doneness, turning once. (Allow 8 to 12 minutes for medium-rare doneness or 12 to 15 minutes for medium doneness.)

To broil: Place steaks on the unheated rack of a broiler pan. Broil with surface of steak 3 to 4 inches from heat to desired doneness, turning once. (Allow 15 to 20 minutes for medium-rare to medium doneness.) Spoon sauce on steaks for the last 2 minutes of broiling.

Beefed-Up Buying

According to surveys on the eating habits of Americans, beef entrées are ordered more often in restaurants than chicken, pork, fish, or seafood. And since 87 percent of consumers say that taste rules their food choices, that must mean people love the taste of beef. As for the form beef takes in lunch and dinner entrées, you probably won't have to think very hard. The hamburger weighs in just ahead of the steak, according to one survey.

Grilled Steaks
with Gorgonzola Butter

The French long have relished steak and pungent, aged cheeses such as Roquefort. If you're a connoisseur of this taste combination, use Gorgonzola cheese. It's more subtle than Roquefort but lends the right character to a flavored butter along with cream cheese and nuts. Top your steaks with the butter as you take them off the grill.

Prep Time: 15 minutes
Grilling Time: 16 minutes

4   boneless beef top loin steaks, cut 1 inch thick
     (about 2 pounds total)
2   tablespoons crumbled Gorgonzola or blue cheese
2   tablespoons soft onion-garlic cream cheese
1   to 2 tablespoons butter, softened
1   tablespoon chopped pine nuts or walnuts, toasted
     Salt
     Thinly sliced fresh basil or chopped parsley

In a grill with a cover arrange preheated coals around a drip pan. Test for medium heat above pan. Place the steaks on the grill rack directly over the drip pan. Cover and grill steaks to desired doneness, turning once. (Allow 16 to 20 minutes for medium-rare doneness or 20 to 24 minutes for medium doneness.)

Meanwhile, for flavored butter, stir together Gorgonzola or blue cheese, cream cheese, butter, and nuts. Shape into 1-inch-diameter log. Wrap in plastic wrap; chill.

Season grilled steaks to taste with salt. Slice flavored butter into 8 slices. Place 1 to 2 slices of flavored butter on each steak. Sprinkle with basil or parsley. Makes 4 servings.

To grill directly: Grill the steaks on the grill rack of an uncovered grill directly over medium coals to desired doneness, turning once. (Allow 8 to 12 minutes for medium-rare doneness or 12 to 15 minutes for medium doneness.)

To broil: Place steaks on the unheated rack of a broiler pan. Broil steaks 3 to 4 inches from heat to desired doneness, turning steaks over once. (Allow 10 to 12 minutes for medium-rare doneness or 16 to 20 minutes for medium doneness.)

Note: If you have any leftover flavored butter, use it as a spread on French bread, on toasted pieces of Italian bread topped with slices of roma tomato, on baked potatoes, or in mashed potatoes.

Bardi's Steak
Dianne Flambé

Total Time: 25 minutes

- 1 10-ounce boneless beef top loin steak,
    cut 1 inch thick
    Salt and pepper
- ¼ teaspoon hot-style mustard
- ¼ cup chopped fresh mushrooms
- ¼ cup chopped green onions
- 3 tablespoons clarified butter*
- 1 tablespoon cognac or brandy
- 2 tablespoons dry red wine
- ¼ cup beef or veal demi-glace
    Several dashes Worcestershire sauce

Trim fat from steak. Butterfly steak by cutting from fatty side almost to opposite side. Sprinkle the steak with salt and pepper. Brush hot-style mustard on 1 side of steak.

In a large skillet cook the mushrooms and green onion in clarified butter until tender. Remove vegetables from skillet. Add steak to skillet. Cook over medium-high heat to desired doneness, turning steak over once. (Allow 3 to 4 minutes for medium-rare doneness or 5 to 6 minutes for medium doneness.)

Meanwhile, in a very small saucepan heat cognac or brandy until it almost simmers. Carefully ignite cognac or brandy and pour it over the steak. Remove steak from skillet. Keep warm. Drain fat from skillet.

Pour wine into skillet. Cook and stir over medium heat until wine evaporates, scraping up any browned bits. Stir in the mushroom mixture, demi-glace, and Worcestershire sauce. Heat through. Return steak to pan. Spoon some of the sauce onto the steak. Fold steak. Top with remaining sauce. Makes 1 serving.
*Note: To clarify butter, in a heavy saucepan melt the butter over low heat without stirring. When the butter is completely melted, you will see a clear, oily layer on top of a milky layer. Slowly pour the clear liquid into a dish, leaving the milky layer in the pan. The clear liquid is the clarified butter.

Bardi's Steak House, located in the heart of Toronto's theater district since 1966, updated this version of a Continental classic. You'll feel like a professional chef handling flaming cognac in the kitchen. If a few guests linger there to watch the preparation—as some always do—they'll be treated to a showstopping experience.

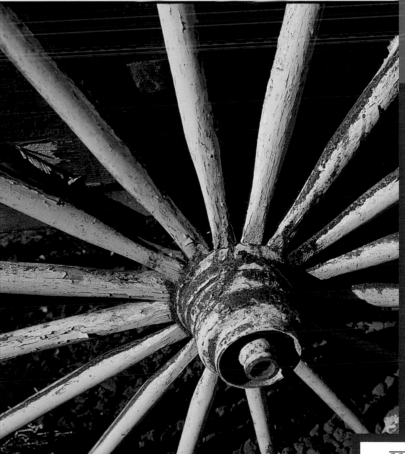

Mediterranean
Steak & Vegetables on Pitas

In Greece and in Turkey where grilling on skewers was born, kabobs are the single greatest loved street food. The marinade for these kabobs infuses sirloin with the herbs and the zest of the Mediterranean. Don't forget the cucumber-yogurt sauce known as *tzatziki*. It's simple yet delicious.

Prep Time: 30 minutes
Marinating Time: 2 to 8 hours
Grilling Time: 5 minutes

- 1   boneless beef top sirloin steak, cut 1 inch thick (about 1½ pounds)
- 2   medium red or green sweet peppers, cut into 1-inch pieces
- 1   medium onion, cut into wedges
- ½   cup Italian salad dressing
- 2   teaspoons dried oregano, crushed
- ½   teaspoon ground black pepper
- ½   cup chopped cucumber
- ½   cup plain yogurt
- 1   clove garlic, minced
- ⅛   teaspoon salt
- 4   large pita bread rounds, warmed

Trim fat from steak. Cut meat into ¼-inch-thick strips. Place the beef strips, sweet pepper pieces, and onion wedges in a plastic bag set in a shallow dish. For marinade, combine salad dressing, oregano, and black pepper. Pour over beef and vegetables, tossing to coat. Close bag. Marinate in refrigerator for at least 2 hours or up to 8 hours.

Meanwhile, for the sauce, stir together the cucumber, yogurt, garlic, and salt. Cover and refrigerate sauce until serving time.

Drain the beef and vegetables, discarding marinade. On 4 long metal skewers thread the beef strips, sweet pepper pieces, and onion wedges, leaving space between pieces. Grill on the rack of an uncovered grill directly over medium coals to desired doneness, turning occasionally. (Allow 5 to 6 minutes for medium doneness.) Serve kabobs with pita rounds and yogurt sauce. Makes 6 servings.

Peppered Beef Tenderloin

Prep Time: 30 minutes
Roasting Time: 30 minutes

3	cloves garlic, minced
1	teaspoon olive oil
2	large portobello mushrooms
2	12-ounce beef tenderloin steaks, cut 1¼ to 1½ inches thick
2	tablespoons snipped fresh rosemary
1	teaspoon salt
1	tablespoon olive oil
2	tablespoons freshly ground white peppercorns
1	tablespoon olive oil
1	recipe Mushroom-Marsala Sauce

In a small bowl stir together garlic and the 1 teaspoon olive oil. Brush portobello mushrooms with the garlic mixture. Place on a rack in a shallow roasting pan. Roast in a 375° oven for 20 to 25 minutes or until mushrooms soften and shrink slightly. Remove from oven. Set aside.

Butterfly each steak by cutting in half horizontally almost through to opposite side. Open each tenderloin. Sprinkle insides with half of the rosemary and half of the salt. Cut mushrooms in half. Place mushrooms inside the tenderloins. Fold tenderloins around mushrooms. Secure meat with short metal or bamboo skewers. Brush meat with the 1 tablespoon olive oil; rub with the remaining rosemary, salt, and the ground white peppercorns.

Pour 1 tablespoon olive oil into an oven-going skillet. Heat over medium-high heat until hot. Add tenderloins. Quickly brown on all sides (about 2 minutes per side).

Place skillet in 375° oven. Roast to desired doneness. (Allow about 30 minutes for medium-rare doneness.)

To serve, cut each tenderloin into 2 pieces. Divide the Marsala-Mushroom Sauce evenly among 4 serving plates. Place 1 piece of tenderloin on top of sauce on each plate. Makes 4 servings.

Mushroom-Marsala Sauce: In a medium saucepan cook ½ cup chopped shallots and 6 cloves minced garlic in 1 tablespoon hot olive oil or cooking oil until tender. Carefully stir in 1 cup dry Marsala and 1 bay leaf. Bring mixture to boiling; reduce heat. Boil gently, uncovered, about 10 minutes or until the mixture is reduced to about ½ cup. Stir in ¾ cup demi-glace or beef broth and ¼ cup half-and-half or light cream. (If the mixture curdles, whisk until smooth.) Return the mixture to boiling; reduce heat. Boil gently, uncovered, about 8 minutes or until the mixture is reduced to about 1 cup. Discard the bay leaf.

Meanwhile, in another saucepan cook 1 cup sliced morel or button mushrooms in 1 tablespoon butter about 3 minutes or until tender. Stir in ¼ cup drained and sliced (oil-pack) dried tomatoes and 1½ teaspoons snipped fresh sage. Stir into the Marsala mixture. Bring to boiling; reduce heat. Stir in 2 tablespoons balsamic vinegar. Season to taste with salt and pepper.

Note: You can start preparing this dish up to 24 hours before serving. Roast the portobello mushrooms according to directions at left. Let mushrooms cool for 30 minutes. Stuff and skewer the tenderloins. Cover and refrigerate for up to 24 hours. Continue as directed.

Here's a recipe that blends the pungency of steak au poivre and the lushness of a Marsala sauce—with a bit of beefy portobello mushroom in every bite. It hails from Chamberlain's Prime Steak and Chop House in Dallas, where Chef Richard Chamberlain serves the tenderloin in high style.

Whisky Steak

Kentuckians claim bourbon as their own. But like many southern traditions, it has strong ties to England and Scotland. In this case, even the spelling of "whisky" sans the "e" harks back to the Mother Tongue. But this recipe comes from the Hereford House in Kansas City. Since 1957 the restaurant has served food that some people refer to as "cowboy cuisine."

Total Time: 25 minutes

- 8   3-ounce beef tenderloin medallions
  Salt and pepper
- 2   tablespoons clarified butter* or cooking oil
- 2   tablespoons finely chopped shallot or yellow onion
- 1   cup beef broth
- ½   cup bourbon
- ½   cup whipping cream
- 1   teaspoon Dijon-style mustard

Lightly sprinkle medallions with salt and pepper. In a 12-inch skillet over medium-high heat, heat butter or oil; add medallions and cook to desired doneness, turning once. (Allow 7 to 9 minutes for medium doneness.) Remove medallions from skillet. Keep warm.

For sauce, reserve 1 tablespoon of the drippings in the skillet; discard remaining drippings. Add shallot or onion. Cook and stir until soft and lightly browned. Carefully add beef broth, then bourbon. Bring to boiling. Boil rapidly, uncovered, for 6 to 8 minutes or until liquid is reduced to ¾ cup. Stir in cream and mustard. Return to boiling. Boil rapidly, uncovered, for 2 to 3 minutes or until liquid is reduced to 1 cup.** (Sauce will thicken enough to coat a spoon.)

Transfer the medallions to 4 serving plates. Pour some of the sauce over medallions; pass remaining sauce. Makes 4 servings.

*Note: To clarify butter, in a heavy saucepan melt the butter over low heat without stirring. When the butter is completely melted, you will see a clear, oily layer on top of a milky layer. Slowly pour the clear liquid into a dish, leaving the milky layer in the pan. The clear liquid is the clarified butter.

**Note: If sauce becomes over-reduced and begins to separate, stir 1 to 2 tablespoons of warm water or beef broth into it to restore consistency.

What's in a Name?

Several cuts of beef have intriguing names, but few cooks know why. Sirloin likely comes from the French word *surlonge* (over the loin). Filet mignon is French for small and boneless; the name first appeared in a book by O. Henry in 1906. It is cut from the small end of the beef tenderloin. London Broil is actually the name of a recipe, not a cut—but some markets sell an appropriate cut (flank, top round, or chuck shoulder) by that name anyway. It's named after England's capital city.

Vic Stewart's
Tender Tips of Filet

Total Time: 50 minutes

1	recipe Onion Gravy
8	ounces pearl onions (about 2 cups)
3	medium carrots, bias-sliced
1½	cups fresh sugar snap pea pods, strings removed
1¼	pounds beef tenderloin, cut into 1 inch pieces
2	tablespoons olive oil
8	ounces mushrooms (such as crimini, oyster, shiitake, or button), coarsely chopped (3 cups)
4	cloves garlic, minced
½	cup dry red wine
4	teaspoons snipped assorted fresh herbs (such as basil, oregano, thyme, rosemary, and tarragon)
	Salt and pepper
10	ounces packaged dried fettuccine, cooked and drained
2	tablespoons butter, melted

Prepare Onion Gravy; keep warm.

Meanwhile, in a medium saucepan cook pearl onions in a small amount of boiling water for 8 to 10 minutes or until just tender. Drain. Cool and peel. Set aside.

In same saucepan cook carrots in a small amount of boiling water about 4 minutes or until nearly crisp-tender. Add sugar snap pea pods; return to boiling and cook 1 to 2 minutes more or until vegetables are crisp-tender. Drain. Set aside; keep vegetables warm.

In a large skillet cook and stir the beef pieces, half at a time, in hot oil over medium-high heat for 3 to 4 minutes or until medium-rare. Remove beef from skillet with slotted spoon. Add mushrooms and garlic to drippings in skillet (add a little additional oil, if necessary). Cook and stir just until tender. Remove mushrooms from skillet. Carefully add wine and herbs to skillet. Cook and stir until bubbly, scraping up any browned bits in skillet. Return meat and mushrooms to skillet. Stir in the Onion Gravy. Heat through. Season to taste with salt and pepper.

Toss together the fettuccine, onions, carrots, sugar snap pea pods, and melted butter. Place in a large serving bowl or on a platter. Top with Onion Gravy mixture. Makes 4 or 5 servings.

Onion Gravy: Slice ½ of a medium red onion and ½ of a medium yellow onion (about 1 cup onion total). In a large saucepan cook onion in 2 tablespoons olive oil over medium-low heat for 10 to 12 minutes or until onion is golden brown. Remove from heat. Carefully stir in ¼ cup brandy, scraping up any browned bits. Add 3½ cups veal stock or two 14½-ounce cans reduced-sodium chicken broth. Bring to boiling; reduce heat. Boil gently, uncovered, for 30 minutes or until reduced to about 2 cups. Cool slightly. Pour mixture, about half at a time, into a blender container or food processor bowl. Cover and blend or process until nearly smooth.* Return mixture to saucepan. Heat until bubbly. Stir together ¼ cup cold water and 3 tablespoons cornstarch. Stir into onion mixture. Cook and stir until thickened and bubbly. Cook and stir for 2 minutes more.

*Note: If desired, prepare gravy ahead up to this point. Cool gravy slightly. Store, covered, in the refrigerator for up to 3 days. At serving time, continue as above.

What Do Ya Call It?

Every time you grill a steak, you are repeating the ritual that gave the food its name. The Saxons and Jutes, who invaded England beginning in the fifth century, brought along their skills as cattlemen. They were master grillers, cooking their beef on pointed sticks over campfires and calling it *steik,* which literally means meat on a stick.

If you're weary of the same old stroganoff, let Vic Stewart's Famous for Steaks of Walnut Creek, California, rebuild the entire flavor profile for you. Actually, this dish was created during the California Gold Rush by hungry miners in Squaw Valley. Chef Robert Mason and John Herrington, owner of Vic Stewart's, proudly present this tasty version.

Grilled Filet Mignon
WITH BLACKENED TOMATO AND OREGANO SAUCE

No, it's not what you think. This tomato isn't "blackened" in the now ubiquitous Cajun style. These bright red delights are charred under a broiler, then mixed into a terrific sauce of oregano and dried pasilla pepper. The combination is a hit at the Capitol Grille of Chicago, an upscale steak and chophouse chain popular in many cities across the country, where big portions are to be expected.

Prep Time: 1 hour
Grilling Time: 8 minutes

- 5   plum tomatoes (about 1 pound)
- 1   dried pasilla pepper
- 2   tablespoons butter
- ½   of a medium onion, finely chopped
- ½   of a medium yellow sweet pepper, chopped
- 1   large clove garlic, minced
- ¼   cup red wine vinegar
- ¼   cup dry white wine
- 1   cup chicken broth or reduced-sodium chicken broth
- 2   tablespoons snipped fresh oregano
- 1   tablespoon snipped fresh thyme
- 6   7-ounce beef tenderloin steaks, cut 1 inch thick
- 2   tablespoons butter

For the sauce, place the tomatoes on the unheated rack of a broiler pan. Broil 3 to 4 inches from the heat for 12 to 14 minutes or until the tomato skins are blistered and begin to blacken, turning occasionally. Transfer tomatoes to a mixing bowl. Cool. Coarsely chop (tomatoes will be soft—do not peel). Set aside.

Wearing rubber or plastic gloves, seed, stem, and finely snip or crumble the pasilla pepper. Set aside.

In a heavy medium saucepan melt 2 tablespoons butter over medium heat; add the onion and cook about 5 minutes or until lightly browned. Add the sweet pepper and garlic. Cook about 4 minutes or until tender. Stir in the red wine vinegar and dry white wine. Bring to boiling, scraping up any browned bits; reduce heat. Simmer, uncovered, about 5 minutes or until liquid is reduced to half of its original volume. Stir in tomatoes, pasilla pepper, and chicken broth. Bring to boiling, reduce heat. Simmer, uncovered, about 15 minutes or until mixture is reduced to 2⅔ cups.

Pour half of the mixture into a blender container or food processor bowl. Cover and blend or process until nearly smooth. Pour into a bowl. Repeat with remaining mixture. Stir in oregano and thyme. If desired, cover and refrigerate until serving time.

Trim any fat from the steaks. Season the steaks with salt and pepper. Grill the steaks on the rack of an uncovered grill directly over medium coals to desired doneness, turning once. (Allow 8 to 12 minutes for medium-rare doneness.)

Before serving, bring the sauce to a simmer; heat through. Remove saucepan from the heat. Whisk in the remaining 2 tablespoons butter. Season sauce with salt and pepper. Place the steaks on serving plates. Serve sauce with the steaks. Makes 6 servings.

Beef Tenderloin
with Wild Mushroom Bordelaise

If you adore an elegant dinner on the spur of the moment, this is the recipe for you. Marlowe's in downtown Denver creates a delectable steak topped with a smooth wild mushroom sauce. And happily, all it takes to make at home is about 35 minutes from start to finish.

Total Time: 35 minutes

2   cups veal stock or reduced-sodium chicken broth
1   cup dry red wine
1   shallot, peeled and chopped
1   bay leaf
1   sprig of thyme, snipped
4   4-ounce beef tenderloin steaks (about 1 inch thick)
1   tablespoon cooking oil
1   cup mixed exotic mushrooms (such as porcini,
       black trumpet, and oyster mushrooms), halved or sliced
1   teaspoon snipped fresh rosemary or ⅛ teaspoon dried
       rosemary, crushed
1   teaspoon butter

In a large saucepan bring veal stock or chicken broth to boiling. Boil rapidly, uncovered, until stock or broth is reduced to 1 cup (about 20 minutes). Meanwhile, in a medium saucepan stir together the red wine, shallot, bay leaf, and thyme. Bring to boiling; reduce heat. Simmer, uncovered, until mixture is reduced to half of its original volume (about 10 to 15 minutes). Stir into broth. Pour through a sieve to strain out solids; discard solids. Set wine mixture aside.

Meanwhile, trim fat from steaks. In a large skillet heat oil over medium-high heat. Add the steaks to the skillet and quickly brown on both sides. Add the mushrooms. Cook and stir until mushrooms are golden brown and steaks are of desired doneness. (Allow 8 to 11 minutes for medium-rare doneness or 12 to 14 minutes for medium doneness.)

Pour wine mixture over steaks and mushrooms. Stir in rosemary and butter. Transfer steaks to a serving platter. Cover and keep warm. Bring the wine mixture to boiling; reduce heat. Simmer, uncovered, for 10 minutes. Serve with the steaks. Makes 4 servings.

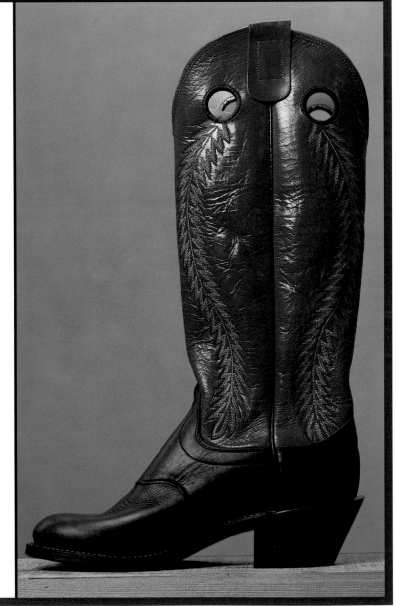

Brandy-Green Peppercorn Sauce

Brandy and green peppercorns make a dynamic duo in a sauce just right for top loin steaks or beef tenderloin. Here from the Sardine Factory (an elegant steak and seafood eatery along John Steinbeck's Cannery Row in Monterey, California) is a deft version. The finished dish is sprinkled with golden brown sautéed pancetta (an Italian bacon). A tasty addition indeed.

Total Time: 25 minutes

¼	cup finely chopped pancetta
1	small shallot, finely chopped
1	clove garlic, minced
2	tablespoons brandy
2	tablespoons dry Madeira
2	tablespoons dry red wine
1½	cups veal stock or reduced-sodium chicken broth
1	tablespoon brandy
1	tablespoon drained whole green peppercorns in brine
	Salt and pepper

In a large skillet cook the pancetta until golden brown. With a slotted spoon, remove pancetta from skillet to a paper towel, reserving drippings in skillet. Cook the shallot and garlic in the drippings in the skillet.

Stir the 2 tablespoons brandy and the Madeira into skillet. Bring to boiling. Boil rapidly for 1 minute. Stir in the red wine. Return to boiling. Boil rapidly for 1 minute. Add veal stock or chicken broth. Bring to boiling; reduce heat. Simmer, uncovered, about 10 minutes or until reduced to half of original volume.

Stir the 1 tablespoon brandy and peppercorns into sauce. Season to taste with salt and pepper. Spoon over steaks. Sprinkle with the pancetta. Makes about ¾ cup sauce.

Grilled Steak
with Martini Twist

You don't need a bartender to concoct this dish. The gin goes in the meat marinade, not a martini glass, and the olive turns up on top of the steak. And don't forget the lemon twist! Now this is one way to put a little class into a steak dinner.

Prep Time: 10 minutes
Marinating Time: 30 minutes
Grilling Time: 16 minutes

4	boneless beef top loin steaks, cut 1 inch thick (about 2 pounds total)
¼	cup finely chopped green onions
¼	cup gin
1	tablespoon olive oil
1	teaspoon finely shredded lemon peel
1	teaspoon tri-colored peppercorns, crushed
	Salt
2	tablespoons sliced pimiento-stuffed green olives
	Lemon twists

Place steaks in a plastic bag set in a shallow dish. For the marinade, stir together the green onions, gin, oil, and lemon peel. Pour the marinade over the steaks. Close the bag. Marinate steaks in the refrigerator for 30 minutes.

Drain the steaks, discarding the marinade.

Press the crushed peppercorns onto both sides of the steaks. In a covered grill arrange preheated coals around a drip pan. Test for medium heat above pan. Place steaks on the grill rack directly over drip pan. Cover and grill to desired doneness. (Allow 16 to 20 minutes for medium-rare doneness or 20 to 24 minutes for medium doneness.) Season to taste with salt. Garnish with sliced olives and lemon twists. Makes 4 servings.

To grill directly: Grill the steaks on the grill rack of an uncovered grill directly over medium-hot coals to desired doneness, turning the steaks once. (Allow 8 to 12 minutes for medium-rare doneness or 12 to 15 minutes for medium doneness.)

To broil: Place the steaks on the unheated rack of a broiler pan. Broil steaks 3 to 4 inches from heat to desired doneness, turning once. (Allow 10 to 12 minutes for medium-rare doneness or 12 to 15 minutes for medium doneness.)

Love It Tenderly

Here's a list of the 10 most tender steaks (listed from most tender to least tender), according to the National Cattlemen's Beef Association:
1. Tenderloin Steak; 2. Chuck Top Blade Steak; 3. Top Loin Steak;
4. Porterhouse/T-Bone Steak; 5. Ribeye Steak; 6. Rib Steak; 7. Chuck Eye Steak;
8. Top Sirloin Steak; 9. Round Tip Steak; and 10. Chopped Steak.

Grilled marinated steak plus salsa and a few other goodies in a bun shouts, "Olé!" The basic steak sandwich boasts a Mexican influence with the use of a simple lime marinade (tortilla fans feel free to use them instead of buns). If you're really adventurous, try the spirited margarita-style sandwich (see note at the end of the recipe) with tequila added to the marinade.

Prep Time: 20 minutes
Marinating Time: 6 to 24 hours
Grilling Time: 12 minutes

1	beef flank steak (1¼ to 1½ pounds)
¼	cup lime juice*
1	tablespoon cooking oil
2	cloves garlic, minced
½	teaspoon ground cumin
	Salt
5	to 6 individual French rolls, warmed
½	cup salsa
2	medium tomatoes, chopped
	Toppings: shredded lettuce, thin strips jicama, dairy sour cream, and/or snipped fresh cilantro (optional)

Score the steak on both sides. Place steak in a plastic bag set in a shallow dish. For marinade, combine lime juice, oil, garlic, and cumin. Pour marinade over steak. Close bag. Marinate the steak in the refrigerator for at least 6 hours or up to 24 hours, turning bag occasionally. Drain steak, discarding the marinade. Season lightly with salt.

Grill the steak on the grill rack of an uncovered grill directly over medium coals to desired doneness, turning once. (Allow 12 to 14 minutes for medium-rare to medium doneness.) Carve steak, across the grain, into thin slices. Place strips on bottoms of French rolls. Top sandwich with salsa, tomatoes, and desired toppings (if using). Place top half of roll on sandwich. Makes 5 to 6 servings.

To grill indirectly: In a grill with a cover arrange preheated coals around a drip pan. Test for medium heat above drip pan. Place the steak on the grill rack directly over the drip pan. Cover; grill to desired doneness. (Allow 18 to 22 minutes for medium-rare to medium doneness.)

To broil: Place steak on unheated rack of a broiler pan. Broil steak about 3 inches from heat to desired doneness, turning steak over once. (Allow 12 to 14 minutes for medium-rare to medium doneness.)

*Note: For a margarita-flavored steak sandwich, reduce the ¼ cup lime juice in the marinade to 2 tablespoons and add ¼ cup tequila.

Taco Steak Sandwich

Vic Stewart's Sierra Nevada
Peppercorn Steak

The secrets to the flavor of this otherwise simple steak dish can be uncovered in two culinary staples: roasted garlic and demi-glace. Chef Robert Mason of Vic Stewart's Famous for Steaks in Walnut Creek, California, shares his secrets for making both. If you want to simplify things in the kitchen, make both the garlic paste and demi-glace a day ahead to cut the final prep time.

Prep Time: 1½ hours
Broiling Time: 11 minutes

- 1 recipe Roasted Garlic Paste
- 1 recipe Sierra Nevada Demi-Glace
- 4 8- to 10-ounce boneless beef top loin steaks, cut 1 inch thick
  Salt
- ¼ cup cracked black peppercorns

Prepare Roasted Garlic Paste. Set aside. Prepare Sierra Nevada Demi-Glace; keep warm.

Trim fat from steaks. Place steaks on the unheated rack of a broiler pan. Broil steaks 3 to 4 inches from the heat to desired doneness, turning steaks once. (Allow 10 to 12 minutes for medium-rare doneness or 12 to 15 minutes for medium doneness.) Season steaks with salt. Generously spread the top of each steak with the Roasted Garlic Paste. Sprinkle each steak with cracked peppercorns. Return steaks to oven; broil for 1 to 2 minutes more or until garlic paste forms a golden brown crust.

Transfer steaks to serving plates. Drizzle each with some of the Sierra Nevada Demi-Glace. (Refrigerate any remaining Demi-Glace; reheat and use within 3 days.) Makes 4 servings.

Roasted Garlic Paste: Peel 8 ounces (6 bulbs) garlic and separate into cloves. Toss garlic cloves with ¼ cup olive oil. Spread in a shallow baking pan. Bake, uncovered, in a 325° oven about 1 hour or until cloves are soft and golden brown, stirring occasionally. Remove from oven. Cool. Place the garlic cloves in a food processor bowl or blender container; add ¼ teaspoon salt and ¼ teaspoon ground black pepper. Cover and process or blend until garlic becomes a paste. (If desired, cover and refrigerate overnight; allow mixture to come to room temperature before using.)

Sierra Nevada Demi-Glace: Finely chop 4 ounces of boneless beef top loin steak. In a large saucepan cook and stir the steak in 3 tablespoons hot olive oil until well browned. Add 1 medium onion, sliced. Cook and stir over medium-high heat until onion is browned. Carefully stir in ½ cup brandy and ¼ cup Sierra Nevada pale ale or other pale ale. Bring to boiling, scraping up any browned bits; reduce heat. Simmer, uncovered, about 5 minutes or until nearly all of the liquid has evaporated. Remove meat chunks with slotted spoon and discard. Stir in two 14½-ounce cans reduced-sodium chicken broth or 3½ cups veal stock. Return to boiling; reduce heat. Simmer, uncovered, about 20 minutes or until mixture is reduced by half. Stir together ¼ cup half-and-half or light cream and 2 tablespoons cornstarch. Add to broth mixture. Cook and stir until thickened and bubbly. Cook and stir for 2 minutes more. Season with salt and pepper. (If desired, cover and refrigerate a day ahead. To serve, cook and stir until bubbly.)

Pineapple Teriyaki Beef

The Japanese flavoring of teriyaki is a natural sidekick to the Hawaiian sweetness of pineapple. The combination starts off first as a marinade for this top round, then does an encore as the sauce over steamed rice. The grated ginger adds just the right Asian zing.

Prep Time: 15 minutes
Marinating Time: 6 to 24 hours
Grilling Time: 24 minutes

- 1 boneless beef top round steak, cut 1½ inches thick (about 2 pounds)
- 1 8-ounce can crushed pineapple (juice pack)
- 2 tablespoons teriyaki sauce
- 2 tablespoons finely chopped green onion
- 2 large cloves garlic, minced
- 1 teaspoon grated fresh gingerroot
  Hot cooked rice (optional)
  Grilled green sweet peppers (optional)

Place steak in a plastic bag set in a shallow dish. Drain pineapple, reserving juice. Cover and refrigerate pineapple. For marinade, combine the reserved pineapple juice, teriyaki sauce, green onion, garlic, and gingerroot. Pour marinade over steak. Close bag. Marinate in the refrigerator for 6 hours or up to 24 hours, turning bag occasionally. Drain the steak, reserving the marinade.

In a grill with a cover arrange preheated coals around a drip pan. Test for medium heat above pan. Place steak on the grill rack directly over drip pan. Cover; grill to desired doneness, turning occasionally. (Allow 24 to 28 minutes for medium-rare doneness.) Cut steak into thin slices.

Meanwhile, in a small saucepan combine the reserved marinade and drained pineapple. Cook and stir over medium heat until slightly thickened and bubbly. If desired, serve steak and sauce with rice and green peppers. Makes 6 to 8 servings.

To broil: Place steak on unheated rack of a broiler pan. Broil with surface of steak 3 to 4 inches from heat to desired doneness, turning once. (Allow 18 to 20 minutes for medium-rare doneness.)

To grill directly: Grill steak on the grill rack of an uncovered grill directly over medium coals to desired doneness, turning occasionally. (Allow 19 to 26 minutes for medium-rare doneness.)

Red-Eye Stew

Prep Time: 20 minutes
Cooking Time: 1½ hours

- 1 pound boneless beef sirloin steak or 1 pound buffalo stew meat
- 2 tablespoons butter or margarine
- 1 small onion, chopped
- ½ cup water
- ¼ cup bourbon
- ¼ cup strong coffee
- 1½ teaspoons Worcestershire sauce
- 4 cloves garlic, minced
- ¾ teaspoon salt
- ¾ teaspoon dried basil, crushed
- ½ teaspoon dried thyme, crushed
- ½ teaspoon dried rosemary, crushed
- ¼ teaspoon pepper
- 2 medium potatoes, peeled and cut into 1-inch cubes
- 1 14½-ounce can diced tomatoes, undrained
- 1½ cups cold water
- ¼ cup all-purpose flour

If using beef sirloin steak, cut into 1-inch pieces. In a Dutch oven brown meat, half at a time, in hot butter or margarine. Return all meat to pan. Stir in the onion, the ½ cup water, the bourbon, coffee, Worcestershire sauce, garlic, salt, basil, thyme, rosemary, and pepper. Bring to boiling; reduce heat. Simmer, covered, for 1 to 1¼ hours or until meat is nearly tender.

Stir in the potatoes. Return to boiling; reduce heat. Simmer, covered, about 25 minutes more or until meat and vegetables are tender. Add the undrained tomatoes. Bring to boiling; reduce heat. Simmer, covered, 5 minutes more.

In a screw-top jar shake together the 1½ cups cold water and the flour; add to Dutch oven. Cook and stir until thickened and bubbly. Cook and stir for 1 minute more. Makes 4 servings (about 5½ cups).

Southerners are known for stirring up "red eye," a ham gravy that often includes coffee as an ingredient. Cooks coined this colorful name because the reddish opening at the center of the reduced sauce looks like an eye. The Buckhorn Exchange, a longtime fixture in Denver, produces its own variation on the theme: Red-Eye Stew— coffee included. Originally built as a brewery warehouse in 1885, the building was converted into a restaurant and saloon in 1893. If you have buffalo meat, use it (as the Exchange does) in place of the beef in this tasty stew.

Korean-Style Barbecued
Flank Steak

One of the most popular Korean dishes is a steak presentation known as *bulgoki*. The marinade ingredients lend a Korean flavor. And don't forget the final sprinkling of sesame seed and green onion.

Prep Time: 10 minutes
Marinating Time: 6 to 24 hours
Grilling Time: 17 minutes

1   beef flank steak (about 1½ pounds)
¼   cup finely chopped green onions
¼   cup soy sauce
2   tablespoons packed brown sugar
1   tablespoon toasted sesame oil
1   tablespoon grated fresh gingerroot
2   large cloves garlic, minced
1   tablespoon sesame seeds, toasted (optional)
   Finely chopped green onion (optional)

Place steak in a plastic bag set in a shallow dish. For marinade, stir together the ¼ cup green onions, soy sauce, brown sugar, sesame oil, gingerroot, and garlic. Pour marinade over steak. Close bag. Marinate in the refrigerator for at least 6 hours or up to 24 hours, turning occasionally. Drain steak, discarding marinade.

Grill steak on the grill rack of an uncovered grill directly over medium coals to desired doneness, turning occasionally. (Allow 17 to 21 minutes for medium-rare to medium doneness.) Carve steak, across the grain, into thin slices. If desired, sprinkle with sesame seeds and additional green onion. Makes 6 servings.

To broil: Place steak on the unheated rack of a broiler pan. Broil steak 2 to 3 inches from heat to desired doneness, turning once. (Allow 13 to 18 minutes for medium-rare to medium doneness.)

London Broil Steak
with Onions and Peppers on Focaccia

Eli's the Place for Steak, just steps off Chicago's Magnificent Mile, creates a fajitalike open-faced steak sandwich, given a solid Mediterranean touch by rosemary focaccia. The marinade packs a lot of flavor into the already enticing London broil. The onions and peppers work well whether grilled or broiled.

Prep Time: 25 minutes
Marinating Time: 6 to 24 hours
Roasting Time: 45 minutes
Standing Time: 10 minutes

1	to 1½ pounds beef flank steak
1	cup olive oil
⅓	cup red wine vinegar
⅓	cup soy sauce
12	garlic cloves, chopped (about ¼ cup)
2	tablespoons snipped fresh parsley
2	tablespoons snipped fresh basil
2	tablespoons snipped fresh thyme
	or 1 teaspoon dried thyme, crushed
1	teaspoon dried oregano, crushed
1	teaspoon paprika
1	teaspoon ground cumin
½	teaspoon ground black pepper
2	red or yellow sweet peppers
2	medium onions
	Nonstick spray coating
2	tablespoons olive oil
	Italian flat bread (focaccia)
	Creamy Dijon-style mustard blend or other
	flavored mustard

Place steak in a plastic bag set in a shallow dish. For marinade, in a medium bowl stir together the 1 cup olive oil, the vinegar, soy sauce, garlic, parsley, basil, thyme, oregano, paprika, cumin, and black pepper. Pour marinade over steak. Close bag. Marinate in refrigerator 6 to 24 hours, turning bag occasionally.

Drain the steak, discarding marinade. Place steak on a rack in a shallow roasting pan. Roast in a 350° oven about 45 minutes or to medium doneness. Allow the steak to stand for 10 minutes before slicing.

While the meat is roasting, remove and discard the stems from sweet peppers; quarter peppers. Remove seeds and membranes; cut into 1-inch-wide strips. Cut onions into eighths. Spray the rack of an unheated broiler pan with nonstick coating. Place the onions and pepper pieces on rack. Brush vegetables with the 2 tablespoons olive oil. While the meat is standing, broil the vegetables 2 to 3 inches from heat for 5 to 8 minutes or until lightly browned.

Thinly slice meat on a diagonal across the grain. In a bowl, combine the meat and vegetables. Serve with flat bread and mustard blend. Makes 6 servings.

Got a Minute?

If you're in a big hurry, we've got the steak for you. The fastest beef in the West (or anywhere else) is a thin-cut, round tip steak, only ⅛ to ¼ inch thick. It cooks in a skillet over medium-high heat in one to two minutes. It's sometimes called a sandwich or breakfast steak, but most prefer the name that gets to the point: minute steak.

Chapter 2

Ribs

Texas-Style

Beef Ribs

The slightly sweet grilling sauce gives a Texas twist to these back ribs. As usual in the Lone Star State, most of the cooking is done before the sauce is slathered on. Be generous with the slathering, however, and be ready to serve more of the sauce on the side.

Prep Time: 25 minutes
Grilling Time: 1 hour

- 3 to 4 pounds beef back ribs (about 8 ribs)*
- 1 teaspoon salt
- 1 teaspoon black pepper
- 1 large onion, finely chopped
- ½ cup honey
- ½ cup catsup
- 1 4-ounce can diced green chili peppers, drained
- 1 tablespoon chili powder
- 1 clove garlic, minced
- ½ teaspoon dry mustard

Trim fat from ribs. For rub, stir together the salt and black pepper. Sprinkle mixture evenly onto both sides of ribs; rub into surface.

In a grill with a cover arrange preheated coals around a drip pan. Test for medium heat above the pan. Place the ribs on the grill rack directly over the drip pan. Cover and grill for 1 to 1¼ hours or until the ribs are tender. Add more coals as needed.

Meanwhile, for sauce, in a small saucepan stir together the onion, honey, catsup, chili peppers, chili powder, garlic, and dry mustard. Cook and stir over low heat for 10 minutes. About 10 minutes before the ribs are finished grilling, brush sauce generously over ribs. Continue grilling until glazed. Pass remaining sauce. Makes 4 servings.

*Note: Ribs may be purchased and grilled either in a rack or cut into individual ribs. If left as a rack, cut into individual pieces to serve.

Spicy Asian-Style

Beef Ribs

Get set for a bit of fire in these wonderful ribs, courtesy of the Chinese hot mustard used in the sauce. If you want to control the heat, mix Dijon-style mustard with ground red pepper instead of using the prepared hot mustard (see recipe note). Whether you grill the ribs individually or as a rack, cut them into smaller pieces before serving them for manageable eating.

Total Prep/Grilling Time: 1 hour, 5 minutes

- 3 to 4 pounds beef back ribs (about 8 ribs)
- ½ cup soy sauce
- ½ cup packed brown sugar or ¼ cup honey
- 5 or 6 cloves garlic, minced
- 3 tablespoons lime or lemon juice
- 4 teaspoons prepared Chinese-style hot mustard*

Trim fat from ribs. In a grill with a cover arrange preheated coals around a drip pan. Test for medium heat above the pan. Place the ribs on the grill rack directly over the drip pan. Cover and grill for 1 to 1¼ hours or until the ribs are tender.

Meanwhile, for sauce, in a small saucepan stir together the soy sauce, brown sugar or honey, garlic, lime or lemon juice, and hot mustard. Bring to boiling; reduce heat. Simmer, uncovered, for 10 minutes or until sauce is slightly thickened, stirring occasionally. Brush ribs once or twice with some of the sauce during the last 10 minutes of grilling. To serve, heat remaining sauce and pass with ribs. Makes 4 servings.

*Note: If you like, use 4 teaspoons Dijon-style mustard plus ⅛ to ¼ teaspoon ground red pepper instead of Chinese-style hot mustard.

K.C. Barbecue

Beef Ribs

These Kansas City-style ribs hail from the K.C. Masterpiece Barbecue and Grill, the eatery spun off from the popular commercial sauce created by grill guru Rich Davis. Made from easily-found ingredients, the sauce is a hit because of the pineapple juice—simply delicious.

Prep Time: 25 minutes
Marinating Time: 4 to 24 hours
Grilling Time: 1¼ hours

- ½ cup cider vinegar
- 3 tablespoons sugar
- 2 teaspoons dry mustard
- ⅛ teaspoon salt
- 2 cups pineapple juice
- ½ cup Worcestershire sauce
- 1 small onion, finely chopped
- 2 tablespoons cooking oil
- 2½ to 3 pounds boneless beef short ribs, cut into serving-size pieces
- 4 teaspoons paprika
- 1½ teaspoons sugar
- 1 teaspoon garlic powder
- ½ teaspoon pepper
- ¼ teaspoon salt
- 4 cups wood chips or 10 to 12 wood chunks (hickory or oak)

For marinade, in a medium saucepan bring the vinegar to boiling. Remove from heat. Stir in the 3 tablespoons sugar, the dry mustard, and the ⅛ teaspoon salt. Stir until sugar is dissolved. Stir in the pineapple juice, Worcestershire sauce, onion, and oil. Cool marinade to room temperature.

Trim fat from ribs. Place ribs in a large plastic bag set in a bowl. Pour marinade over ribs. Close bag. Marinate in the refrigerator for at least 4 hours or up to 24 hours, turning bag occasionally.

Meanwhile, for rub, in a small mixing bowl stir together the paprika, the 1½ teaspoons sugar, the garlic powder, pepper, and the ¼ teaspoon salt.

At least 1 hour before smoke-cooking, soak wood chips (for the grill method) or wood chunks (for the smoker method) in enough water to cover.

Remove ribs from marinade. Pat dry with paper towels. Generously sprinkle both sides of ribs with the paprika mixture; rub mixture into ribs.

Drain wood chips. In a grill with a cover arrange preheated coals around a drip pan. Test for medium heat above the pan. Sprinkle one-fourth of the drained chips over the coals. If desired, place the ribs in a rib rack. Place the ribs on the grill rack directly over the drip pan. Cover and grill the ribs for 1¼ hours or until tender. Add more drained chips every 15 minutes and more coals as needed. Makes 6 to 8 servings.

Smoker method: Drain wood chunks. In a smoker arrange preheated coals, drained wood chunks, and water pan according to manufacturer's directions. Pour water into pan. If desired, place ribs in a rib rack. Place ribs on the grill rack over the water pan. Cover and grill ribs for 4 to 5 hours or until tender.

Braised BBQ
Beef Short Ribs

Prep Time: 15 minutes
Cooking Time: 1 hour, 40 minutes

3	pounds beef short ribs or
	2 pounds boneless beef short ribs
½	teaspoon salt
1	15-ounce can Italian-style tomato sauce
1	small onion, chopped
1	tablespoon Worcestershire sauce
¼	teaspoon ground cinnamon
¼	teaspoon pepper

Trim fat from ribs. Place ribs in 4-quart Dutch oven; add enough water to cover ribs. Add the salt. Bring to boiling; reduce heat. Simmer, covered, about 1½ hours for bone-in ribs or 1¼ hours for boneless ribs or until meat is very tender. Remove ribs from Dutch oven. Drain ribs; set aside.

For sauce, wipe out Dutch oven. In the Dutch oven combine the tomato sauce, onion, Worcestershire sauce, cinnamon, and pepper. Bring sauce mixture to boiling; add the ribs. Return to boiling; reduce heat. Simmer, covered, for 10 minutes, gently stirring and spooning sauce over ribs occasionally. Makes 6 to 8 servings.

Making the Grade

While beef inspection by the federal government is mandatory to guarantee safety, grading of beef is not. It's optional and paid for by the beef industry. Meat is graded by the U.S. Department of Agriculture according to "palatability." The higher the grade, the more marbling and the better the quality. The three grades used in retail include Prime (highest quality), Choice (second-highest), and Select (midlevel quality).

Braising is a way of keeping meat moist throughout the cooking process. Count on your Dutch oven to render these tender ribs. For the final touch, make the cinnamon-spiced sauce, add the cooked ribs, and simmer just long enough to glaze the ribs with sauce.

Chutney

Although primarily associated with foods of India, chutney—a vinegar, spice, and fruit-based mixture—has become a versatile sidekick to just about any cuisine. In this recipe, the chutney is cut or snipped into smaller pieces using kitchen shears. That's to create a salsa that will, in this case, literally stick to your ribs during grilling.

Spareribs

Prep Time: 20 minutes
Cook Time: 1 hour
Grilling Time: 15 minutes

- 3 to 4 pounds meaty pork spareribs or loin back ribs
  Salt
- 1 cup snipped chutney
- ¼ cup bottled chili sauce
- 2 tablespoons vinegar
- 1 tablespoon Worcestershire sauce
- 1 teaspoon dry mustard
- ½ teaspoon onion powder
  Several dashes bottled hot pepper sauce
- 1 tablespoon water

Trim fat from ribs. Cut ribs into serving-size pieces. Place ribs in a Dutch oven. Add enough water to cover the ribs. Bring to boiling; reduce the heat. Simmer, covered, about 1 hour or until meat is tender. Drain the ribs. Sprinkle with salt.

For sauce, in a medium saucepan combine the chutney, chili sauce, vinegar, Worcestershire sauce, dry mustard, onion powder, hot pepper sauce, and the 1 tablespoon water. Cook and stir over medium heat until heated through.

Place ribs, meaty sides down, on the rack of an uncovered grill directly over medium coals. Grill 10 minutes. Turn the ribs meaty side up; brush with some of the sauce. Grill 5 minutes more. Pass remaining warmed sauce. Makes 6 servings.

Plum-Sauced

Spareribs

In Chinese cooking, one of the most delicate and beloved components is plum sauce, used to good effect in such dishes as Peking duck and moo shu pork. Here—homemade using canned plums—the sauce becomes a glaze for pork spareribs. The sesame seeds add welcome texture to the sauce.

Prep Time: 30 minutes
Grilling Time: 1¼ hours

1   16-ounce can whole unpitted purple plums
2   tablespoons frozen orange juice concentrate, thawed
2   tablespoons bottled hoisin sauce
1   tablespoon soy sauce
1   teaspoon grated fresh gingerroot
¼   teaspoon pepper
2   tablespoons sesame seed, toasted
4   pounds pork spareribs, cut into serving-size pieces
    Salt and pepper

For sauce, drain plums, reserving liquid. Pit plums. In a food processor bowl or blender container combine the pitted plums, reserved plum liquid, the orange juice concentrate, hoisin sauce, soy sauce, gingerroot, and pepper. Cover and process or blend until mixture is nearly smooth. Transfer the mixture to a saucepan. Bring to boiling; reduce heat. Simmer, uncovered, about 15 minutes or until slightly thickened. Stir in the sesame seed.

Trim fat from ribs. Sprinkle ribs with salt and pepper. In a grill with a cover arrange preheated coals around a drip pan. Test for medium heat above the pan. If desired, place ribs in a rib rack. Place the ribs on the grill directly over the drip pan. Cover and grill for 1¼ to 1½ hours or until ribs are tender. Add more coals as needed. Brush with sauce the last 10 minutes of grilling. Heat any remaining sauce and pass with the ribs. Makes 6 servings.

Strawberry-Jalapeño
Barbecue Ribs

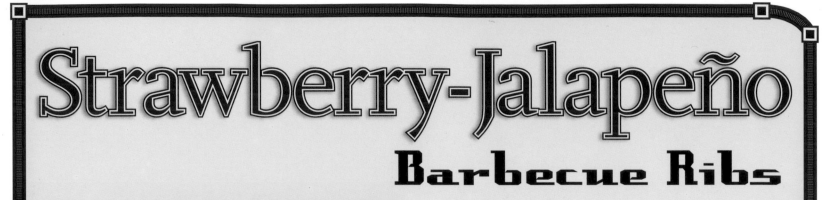

Prep Time: 20 minutes
Grilling Time: 1¼ hours

- ¼ cup chopped onion
- 1 clove garlic, minced
- 1 tablespoon cooking oil
- ½ cup catsup
- ½ cup strawberry preserves or strawberry jam
- ¼ cup cider vinegar or beer
- 1 or 2 jalapeño peppers, seeded and finely chopped
- 1 tablespoon bottled steak sauce
- 1 teaspoon chili powder
- 3 pounds pork loin back ribs
- ½ teaspoon ground cumin
- ¼ teaspoon garlic salt
- ⅛ to ¼ teaspoon ground red pepper

For sauce, in a small saucepan cook the onion and garlic in hot oil until tender. Stir in the catsup, strawberry preserves or jam, vinegar or beer, jalapeño peppers, steak sauce, and chili powder. Bring just to boiling; reduce heat. Simmer, uncovered, about 10 minutes or until mixture thickens slightly, stirring occasionally. Set aside.

Trim fat from ribs. In a small mixing bowl stir together the cumin, garlic salt, and red pepper. Sprinkle cumin mixture evenly over both sides of ribs; rub into surface.

Cut ribs into serving-size pieces. In a grill with a cover arrange preheated coals around a drip pan. Test for medium heat above the pan. If desired, place ribs in a rib rack. Place ribs on the grill rack directly over the drip pan. Cover and grill for 1¼ to 1½ hours or until the ribs are tender. Add more coals as needed. Brush ribs with the sauce occasionally during the last 10 minutes of grilling. Heat the remaining sauce until bubbly; serve with the ribs. Makes 6 servings.

Pork and fruit sauces please palates nationwide. For a surprising fruit sauce to complement any kind of pork you fancy, combine the sweetness of strawberry preserves (an easy base for sauces) with fiery jalapeños for a definite Southwest sensation.

Rhubarb-Glazed
Baby Back Ribs

Unless you are Pennsylvania Dutch or have a deep fondness for rhubarb pie, you may never have used the fruit of this long-stalked plant. When eaten au naturel, this blushed-rose fruit is tart. Here it is sweetened with cranberry-apple juice for a saucy glaze that is definitely worth a try.

Prep Time: 35 minutes
Grilling Time: 45 minutes

3	to 3½ pounds pork loin back ribs or meaty pork spareribs
½	teaspoon onion salt
½	teaspoon pepper
1	recipe Rhubarb Glaze

Trim fat from ribs. Cut the ribs into serving-size pieces; place in a Dutch oven. Add enough water to cover the ribs. Bring to boiling; reduce heat. Simmer, covered, for 30 minutes. Drain ribs; cool slightly. Season the ribs with the onion salt and pepper.

In a covered grill arrange preheated coals around a drip pan. Test for medium heat above drip pan. If desired, place precooked ribs in a rib rack. Place the ribs on the grill rack directly over the drip pan. Cover and grill for 45 to 50 minutes or until ribs are tender, brushing occasionally with Rhubarb Glaze during the last 10 minutes of grilling. Heat the remaining glaze on the grill or rangetop until bubbly; pass with the ribs. Makes 4 servings.

Rhubarb Glaze: In a 2-quart saucepan combine 4 cups sliced fresh or frozen rhubarb and half of a 12-ounce can frozen cranberry-apple juice cocktail concentrate. Bring to boiling; reduce heat. Simmer glaze, covered, about 15 minutes or until rhubarb is very tender. Strain mixture into a 2-cup liquid measure, pressing out liquid with the back of a spoon. If necessary, add enough water to measure 1¼ cups liquid. Discard the pulp.

In the same saucepan combine 2 tablespoons cornstarch and 2 tablespoons cold water. Stir in the strained liquid. Cook and stir until thickened and bubbly. Cook 2 minutes more. Stir in ⅓ cup honey, 2 tablespoons Dijon-style mustard, and 1 tablespoon wine vinegar. Heat through. Use about half of the glaze for the ribs. Cool, cover, and store the remaining glaze in the refrigerator; use within 5 days. Makes 1¾ cups.

Right in the Ribs

Pork ribs come in five basic types. Each has a passionate following among cooks. Here's what's in the market so you can determine your favorite too.

Back ribs, cut from the blade and center section of the loin, contain bones and "finger meat" in between. Spareribs hail from the underbelly or side. St. Louis-style ribs are spareribs with the breast bone removed. Country style are the meatiest pork ribs; you'll need a knife and fork for these. And yes, there are even boneless pork "ribs," cut creatively from a loin or chop. Is this a great country, or what?

Sweet and Spicy
BBQ Ribs

Americans favor sweet and spicy, so these pork loin back ribs should develop quite a fan club. The catsup and brown sugar kick in the sweet, while the curry powder brings both a bright yellow color and a mix of 13 to 19 blended spices, depending on the curry powder you buy.

Prep Time: 35 minutes
Grilling Time: 1½ hours

1½ cups catsup
¾ cup white wine vinegar
½ cup packed brown sugar
2 tablespoons curry powder
1 tablespoon Worcestershire sauce
1 teaspoon hickory-flavored salt
1 teaspoon pepper
2 or 3 cloves garlic, minced
3½ or 4 pounds pork loin back ribs

In a large bowl combine the catsup, vinegar, brown sugar, curry powder, Worcestershire sauce, hickory-flavored salt, pepper, and garlic. Cover; let stand at room temperature for 30 minutes or refrigerate for up to 5 days.

In a covered grill arrange preheated coals around a drip pan. Test for medium heat above the pan. If desired, place ribs in rib rack. Place ribs on the grill rack directly over the drip pan. Cover and grill for 1½ to 2 hours or until ribs are very tender. Add more coals as needed. Brush generously with sauce during the last 15 minutes of grilling. Makes 8 servings.

Southwestern Ribs

Think Southwest, and it's easy to conjure up images of cowpokes cooking ribs under starry skies after a long day on the ranch. Give these ribs southwestern character with mesquite, cumin, red pepper, and a nifty dried herb rub (conveniently made in a food processor or blender).

Soaking Time (for chips): 1 hour
Total Prep/Grilling Time: 1½ hours

4	cups mesquite wood chips
1	cup catsup
½	cup light-colored corn syrup
¼	cup white vinegar
¼	cup packed brown sugar
¼	cup finely chopped onion
2	tablespoons prepared mustard
1½	teaspoons Worcestershire sauce
2	cloves garlic, minced
½	teaspoon coarsely ground black pepper
½	teaspoon bottled hot pepper sauce
¼	teaspoon ground cumin or chili powder
⅛	teaspoon ground red pepper
4	pounds pork loin back ribs
1	recipe Herb Rub

At least 1 hour before grilling, soak wood chips in enough water to cover.

In a 1½-quart saucepan combine the catsup, corn syrup, vinegar, brown sugar, onion, mustard, Worcestershire sauce, garlic, black pepper, hot pepper sauce, cumin or chili powder, and red pepper. Bring mixture to boiling; reduce heat. Simmer, uncovered, for 25 to 30 minutes or until the mixture is thickened, stirring occasionally.

Trim fat from ribs. Cut the ribs into serving-size pieces. Sprinkle the Herb Rub evenly onto both sides of the ribs; rub mixture onto the ribs.

In a grill with a cover arrange preheated coals around a drip pan. Test for medium heat above the pan. Sprinkle some of the drained wood chips over the coals. If desired, place ribs in rib rack. Place the ribs on the grill rack directly over the drip pan. Cover and grill for 1¼ to 1½ hours or until the ribs are tender. Add more wood chips every 15 minutes and more coals as needed. Brush with some of the sauce during the last 10 minutes of grilling. Pass any additional sauce. Makes 6 servings.

Herb Rub: In a blender container or small food processor bowl combine 2 teaspoons dried rosemary, 2 teaspoons dried thyme, 2 teaspoons dried minced onion, 2 teaspoons dried minced garlic, 1 teaspoon coarse salt, and ¾ teaspoon ground black pepper. Blend or process until coarsely ground.

That Thing You Don't

Pork does not have to be overcooked (read: dry) to be safe. It should be cooked only to medium to preserve its tenderness and juiciness. Overcooking destroys both qualities, producing a tough, tasteless piece of meat that gets robbed of its true juicy character. If you're cooking a roast, use a meat thermometer and check for an internal temperature reading of 160°. If you're cooking a smaller cut, look for a blush of pink and plenty of savory clear juices.

Jack's Hot Sauce

Sure, there are plenty of bottles on the shelf proclaiming themselves as hot sauce. But if you're really after some hot stuff, try this recipe from Jack Cawthon of Jack's Bar-B-Que on Broadway—in Nashville, that is. Black pepper, red pepper, and hot chili powder lend the sizzle to the sauce. It's not recommended for the meek of tongue.

Prep Time: 15 minutes
Cooking Time: 8 minutes

- 2 cups catsup
- ½ cup golden syrup or dark-colored corn syrup
- 2 tablespoons brown sugar
- 1 tablespoon lemon juice
- 2½ teaspoons hot chili powder
- 2 teaspoons dried minced onion
- ½ teaspoon ground black pepper
- ¼ to ½ teaspoon ground red pepper
- ¼ teaspoon salt

In a medium saucepan combine the catsup, syrup, brown sugar, lemon juice, chili powder, minced onion, black pepper, red pepper, and salt. Cook, stirring occasionally, until mixture just boils; reduce heat. Simmer, uncovered, for 8 minutes. Serve on grilled pork chops, grilled ribs, or hamburgers. Makes about 2½ cups.

RIB Sandwich $4.75

Country Ribs
with Peach Jalapeño Sauce

Prep Time: 15 minutes
Grilling Time: 1½ hours

1   to 2 fresh jalapeño peppers
1   15- to 16-ounce can peach slices, drained
½   cup chopped onion
¼   cup light-colored corn syrup
2   tablespoons bottled steak sauce
¼   teaspoon ground cumin
½   cup peach chutney
2½ to 3 pounds pork country-style ribs

Wearing plastic or rubber gloves, quarter the jalapeño peppers and remove stems, seeds, and veins. Finely chop peppers. Set aside.

For sauce, in a blender container or food processor bowl combine the peach slices, onion, corn syrup, steak sauce, and cumin. Cover and blend or process until nearly smooth. Pour into a small saucepan. Stir in the chutney and chopped jalapeño peppers. Cook and stir over low heat until heated through.

Trim fat from ribs. In a grill with a cover arrange preheated coals around a drip pan. Test for medium heat above the pan. Place the ribs on grill rack directly over drip pan. Cover and grill for 1½ to 2 hours or until ribs are tender. Add more coals as needed. Brush 2 or 3 times with the peach mixture during the last 10 minutes of grilling. Heat any remaining sauce until bubbly; serve with ribs. Makes 4 servings.

If you love pork, peaches, and convenience, this is the recipe of choice. What could be easier than opening up a can of sweet golden peaches, blending them up real smooth, then adding peach chutney and a little kick of jalapeño peppers?

Mustard-Glazed Ribs

Prep Time: 20 minutes
Grilling Time: 1½ hours

⅓ cup chopped onion
2 tablespoons olive oil or
    cooking oil
1 8-ounce jar spicy
    brown mustard
2 tablespoons honey
2 tablespoons cider vinegar
¼ teaspoon ground red pepper
⅛ teaspoon ground cloves
2½ to 3 pounds pork
    country-style ribs

For glaze, in a saucepan cook
onion in hot oil until tender.
Stir in mustard, honey, vinegar,
red pepper, and cloves. Bring to
boiling; reduce heat. Simmer,
uncovered, for 5 minutes,
stirring occasionally.

Trim fat from ribs. In a grill
with a cover arrange preheated
coals around a drip pan. Test
for medium heat above pan.
Place ribs on grill rack directly
over drip pan. Cover and grill
for 1½ to 2 hours or until ribs
are tender. Add more coals as
needed. Brush the ribs
frequently with glaze during
the last 10 minutes of grilling.
Makes 4 servings.

Mustard gives this balanced sweet and sour glaze a real flavor punch. If you want to make dining memorable, embellish pork ribs with this straightforward glaze. It takes just 20 minutes or less to make. Even better, you probably have all the ingredients on hand.

Apple Butter Ribs

Apple butter, a Pennsylvania Dutch dish made by pureeing apples with apple cider, has been an American institution since the 1700s. In this recipe, its light sweetness provides just the right counterpoint to the vinegar and horseradish mustard.

Prep Time: 15 minutes
Grilling Time: 1½ hours

1	cup apple butter
2	tablespoons vinegar
1	teaspoon horseradish mustard
½	teaspoon celery seed
¼	teaspoon sugar
¼	teaspoon salt
¼	teaspoon garlic powder
⅛	teaspoon pepper
2½ to 3 pounds pork country-style ribs	

For sauce, in a small saucepan stir together the apple butter, vinegar, mustard, celery seed, sugar, salt, garlic powder, and pepper. Bring just to boiling, stirring often.

Trim fat from the ribs. In a covered grill arrange preheated coals around a drip pan. Test for medium heat above the pan. Place the ribs on the grill rack directly over the drip pan. Cover and grill for 1½ to 2 hours or until ribs are tender. Add more coals as needed. Brush the ribs occasionally with the sauce during the last 15 minutes of grilling. Heat any remaining sauce; pass with the ribs. Makes 4 servings.

Oven-Roasted

Ribs with Maple Barbecue Sauce

So what if your outdoor grill is being dowsed by a storm outside the door. You can make these first-rate country-style ribs without letting a single raindrop fall on your head. It's easy because you bake them in the oven. You'll be happy and dry.

Prep Time: 25 minutes
Baking Time: 1¾ hours

2½ to 3 pounds pork country-style ribs
¾ cup catsup
⅓ cup maple-flavored syrup
2 tablespoons cider vinegar
1 tablespoon bottled steak sauce
1 tablespoon prepared mustard or
    Dijon-style mustard
1 teaspoon ground cinnamon
¼ teaspoon ground allspice
¼ teaspoon ground black pepper
⅛ teaspoon ground cloves
    Several dashes bottled hot pepper sauce

Line a shallow roasting pan with foil. Place ribs, bone sides up, in the prepared pan. Bake in a 350° oven for 1 hour. Drain off fat. Turn ribs meaty sides up.

Meanwhile, for the sauce, in a small saucepan stir together the catsup, maple syrup, vinegar, steak sauce, mustard, cinnamon, allspice, black pepper, cloves, and hot pepper sauce. Bring to boiling; reduce heat. Simmer, uncovered, for 15 minutes.

Spoon half of the sauce over the ribs. Bake, covered, for 45 to 60 minutes more or until ribs are tender, adding the remaining sauce the last 15 minutes. Makes 4 servings.

Roasted Pork Ribs with
Cranberry Salsa

Hardly ordinary, cranberries grow on low, trailing vines in sandy bogs. Unfortunately, the peak time of availability for these scarlet-colored gems is only a short few months—October through December. But thanks to the wonders of preserving cranberries in a can, you are able to enjoy these ribs slathered with this fruity salsa any time of year.

Prep Time: 10 minutes
Baking Time: 1 hour, 40 minutes

3	pounds boneless pork country-style ribs
	Salt and pepper
¾	cup picante sauce
¾	cup whole cranberry sauce (about ½ of a 16-ounce can)
1½	teaspoons finely shredded orange peel
¼	cup orange juice
1	teaspoon snipped fresh mint or ½ teaspoon dried mint, crushed

Trim fat from ribs. Season ribs with salt and pepper. Place ribs in a 13x9x2-inch baking pan. Cover with foil. Bake in a 350° oven for 1 hour. Drain off fat.

Meanwhile, stir together the picante sauce, cranberry sauce, orange peel, orange juice, and mint. Spoon sauce over the meat. Bake, uncovered, about 40 minutes more or until ribs are tender, spooning sauce over meat occasionally. Makes 6 servings.

Piquant Ribs

Pungent with the flavors of mustard, curry, vinegar, and liquid smoke, these ribs can only be described as being piquant. First, a spice mixture is rubbed onto the ribs. After having time to "ripen" and absorb the flavors, the ribs are then grilled. The mustard-and-honey sauce brings it all together for a memorable combination of tastes.

Prep Time: 40 minutes
Marinating Time: 2 to 6 hours
Grilling Time: 1¼ hours

⅓ cup granulated sugar
1 teaspoon pepper
2 teaspoons paprika
1 teaspoon curry powder
½ teaspoon salt
3½ to 4 pounds pork country-style ribs
1 cup packed brown sugar
⅔ cup white vinegar or cider vinegar
½ cup chopped onion
⅓ cup spicy brown mustard or Dijon-style mustard
2 cloves garlic, minced
2 tablespoons honey
2 teaspoons liquid smoke
¼ teaspoon celery seed

In a small mixing bowl combine the granulated sugar, pepper, paprika, curry powder, and salt. Rub over ribs, coating well. Place the ribs in a shallow pan. Cover and refrigerate for 2 to 6 hours.

In a covered grill arrange medium coals around a drip pan. Test for medium-low heat above pan. Place ribs, fat side up, on grill rack over drip pan but not over coals. Lower grill hood. Grill about 1¼ hours or until tender, turning once and adding more coals as needed.

Meanwhile, for sauce, in a medium saucepan combine the brown sugar, vinegar, onion, mustard, garlic, honey, liquid smoke, and celery seed. Bring to boiling; reduce heat. Cook sauce, uncovered, for 25 to 30 minutes or until slightly thickened, stirring occasionally.

Brush sauce over ribs occasionally during the last 10 to 15 minutes of grilling. Heat any remaining sauce until bubbly and pass with the ribs. Makes 8 servings.

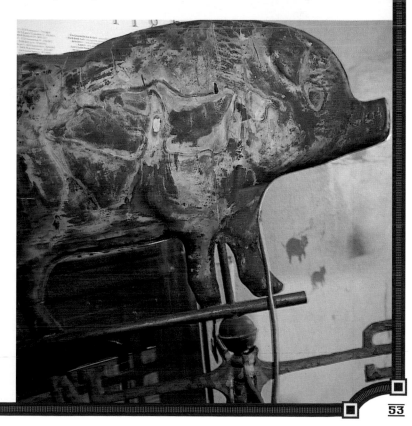

Chapter 3

CHOPS

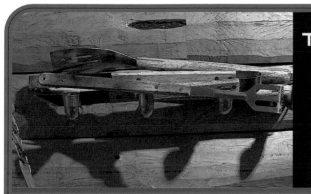

This Provençal-influenced rendition of lamb chops draws on two famous flavorings: garlic and rosemary. As for the mustard, a coarse grain is called for but with so many flavored mustards available, give another a try if you like.

Garlic ～ Rosemary

Grilled Lamb Chops

Prep Time: 10 minutes
Grilling Time: 16 minutes

- 8 lamb rib or loin chops, cut 1 inch thick (about 2½ pounds total)
- 2 tablespoons coarse-grain brown mustard
- 2 cloves garlic, minced
- 1 tablespoon snipped fresh rosemary or 1 teaspoon dried rosemary, crushed
- ½ teaspoon cracked black pepper
- 1½ teaspoons snipped fresh thyme or ½ teaspoon dried thyme, crushed

Trim fat from chops. Spread both sides of chops with the mustard. In a bowl stir together garlic, rosemary, pepper, and thyme. Press mixture evenly onto both sides of chops.

In a grill with a cover arrange preheated coals around a drip pan. Test for medium heat above the pan. Place the chops on grill rack directly over pan. Cover and grill to desired doneness. (Allow 16 to 18 minutes for medium-rare doneness or 18 to 20 minutes for medium doneness.) Makes 4 servings.

Jellied cranberry sauce joins forces with apricot or peach to make a nice basting sauce for pork chops. Lemon juice or cider vinegar helps balance the sweetness, while the chipotles (smoked and dried jalapeños) add a little heat.

Cranberry
Chipotle Pork Chops

Total Prep and Grilling Time: 40 minutes

- 4 pork loin rib chops, cut 1¼ inches thick (about 3 pounds total)
- 1 8-ounce can jellied cranberry sauce
- ⅓ cup apricot or peach preserves or apricot or peach spreadable fruit
- ¼ cup chopped onion
- 1 tablespoon lemon juice or cider vinegar
- 1 canned chipotle pepper in adobo sauce or 1 jalapeño pepper, seeded and chopped

Trim any fat from the pork chops. In a grill with a cover arrange the preheated coals around a drip pan. Test for medium heat above the drip pan. Place the pork chops on the grill rack directly over the drip pan. Cover and grill the chops for 35 to 40 minutes or until the juices run clear.

Meanwhile, for sauce, in a small saucepan combine the cranberry sauce, preserves or spreadable fruit, onion, lemon juice or vinegar, and pepper. Bring to boiling, stirring constantly; reduce heat. Simmer, uncovered, for 5 minutes, stirring occasionally.

To serve, brush the chops with sauce. Pass remaining sauce with chops. Makes 4 servings.

To broil: Prepare sauce and pork chops as directed above, except instead of grilling place pork chops on the unheated rack of a broiler pan. Broil with the surface of the chops 3 to 4 inches from the heat for 18 to 22 minutes or until juices run clear, turning once. Serve as above.

Pork Slims Down

Now that pigs are bred to be trimmer, the long-used expression "eating like a pig" doesn't seem to apply anymore. For one thing, today's pork is 31 percent lower in fat than it was a decade ago, with 14 percent fewer calories and 10 percent less cholesterol. For another, there's a new emphasis on closer-trimmed, more carefully prepared pork. A 3-ounce portion of roasted pork tenderloin weighs in with the same calorie count (139) as a roasted skinless chicken breast, with only slightly more total fat and slightly less cholesterol. Such a loss truly is everybody's gain.

The thick, dark, malty ale known as stout is the centerpiece of the marinade for these thick-cut pork chops. Mixing it with honey mustard brings a signature flavor to this dish, perfect for the outdoor grill or the indoor broiler.

Stout-Glazed
Pork Chops

Prep Time: 30 minutes
Marinating Time: 6 to 24 hours
Grilling Time: 30 minutes

4   boneless pork top loin chops, cut 1¼ inches thick
      (about 1¾ pounds total)
1   12-ounce bottle stout
½   cup chopped onion
¼   cup honey mustard
3   cloves garlic, minced
1   teaspoon caraway seed
      Salt and pepper

Trim fat from the chops. Place chops in a plastic bag set in a shallow dish. For the marinade, stir together the stout, onion, honey mustard, garlic, and caraway seed. Pour the marinade over chops. Close bag. Marinate chops in the refrigerator for at least 6 hours or up to 24 hours, turning the bag occasionally.

Drain the chops, reserving marinade. Sprinkle chops with salt and pepper. Pour marinade into a small saucepan. Bring to boiling; reduce heat. Simmer, uncovered, about 15 minutes or until the marinade is reduced by about half.

Meanwhile, in a grill with a cover arrange preheated coals around a drip pan. Test for medium heat above the pan. Place chops on grill rack directly over drip pan. Cover and grill for 30 to 35 minutes or until the juices run clear, brushing chops frequently with marinade during the last 10 minutes of grilling. Discard any remaining marinade. Makes 4 servings.

To broil: Prepare marinade and chops as directed, except place chops on the unheated rack of a broiler pan. Broil with surface of chops 3 to 4 inches from the heat for 18 to 22 minutes or until juices run clear, turning once and brushing frequently with marinade the last 10 minutes of broiling. Discard any remaining marinade.

Corn Bread~Stuffed Chops

Prep Time: 25 minutes
Grilling Time: 35 minutes

- 3 cups apple or cherry wood chips
- ¼ teaspoon ground black pepper
- ⅛ teaspoon celery seed
- ⅛ teaspoon onion salt or garlic salt
  Dash ground cloves
  Dash ground red pepper (optional)
- ¼ pound bulk pork sausage or bulk turkey sausage
- ¼ cup chopped onion
- ½ cup corn bread stuffing mix
- ¼ cup dried cranberries
- ½ of a 4-ounce can diced green chili peppers, drained
- 2 tablespoons snipped fresh parsley
- 1 to 2 tablespoons apple juice, chicken broth, or water
- 4 pork loin rib chops, cut 1½ inches thick
  (about 3 pounds total)

At least 1 hour before cooking, soak wood chips in enough water to cover.

For the seasoning rub, stir together the black pepper, celery seed, onion or garlic salt, cloves, and red pepper (if using).

For stuffing, in a small saucepan cook the sausage and onion until sausage is no longer pink and onion is tender. Drain off fat. Stir in the stuffing mix, cranberries, chili peppers, and parsley. Add enough of the apple juice, broth, or water to just moisten.

Trim fat from pork chops. Cut a pocket in each chop by cutting a slit in the fatty side and working the knife inside to cut almost to bone (keep original slit small). Spoon stuffing into pockets in chops. If necessary, secure with wooden picks. Sprinkle the seasoning rub evenly over both sides of the pork chops; rub in.

Drain the wood chips. In a grill with a cover arrange preheated coals around a drip pan. Test for medium heat above the pan. Sprinkle half of the drained chips over the coals. Place chops on the grill rack directly over the drip pan. Cover and grill chops for 35 to 40 minutes or until the juices run clear, turning chops once. Add more wood chips every 15 minutes.

If using wooden picks, remove the picks before serving. Makes 4 servings.

The way to any southerner's heart is through his corn bread. This recipe takes corn bread stuffing a step further with the addition of sausage, onions, and cranberries. And don't underestimate the flavor contribution of the apple or cherry wood placed on the hot coals.

You can use tequila or just fresh lime juice to make the marinade. Either way, the taste is reminiscent of Mexico's most beloved cocktail, the margarita. In this Margaritaville, however, no pork chops will be left to waste away again.

BOOT CITY ★

Margarita~Glazed
Pork Chops

Prep Time: 10 minutes
Grilling Time: 12 minutes

4 boneless pork loin chops, cut 1 inch thick
(about 1½ pounds total)
⅓ cup orange marmalade
1 jalapeño pepper, seeded and finely chopped
2 tablespoons tequila or lime juice
1 teaspoon grated fresh gingerroot or
½ teaspoon ground ginger
Snipped fresh cilantro
Lime and orange wedges (optional)

Trim fat from the pork chops. For glaze, in a small mixing bowl stir together the orange marmalade, jalapeño pepper, tequila or lime juice, and gingerroot or ginger. Place the pork chops on the rack of an uncovered grill directly over medium coals for 12 to 15 minutes or until juices run clear, turning chops once and frequently brushing with glaze during the last 5 minutes of grilling. To serve, sprinkle with cilantro. If desired, garnish with lime and orange wedges. Makes 4 servings.

To grill indirectly: In a grill with a cover arrange preheated coals around a drip pan. Test for medium heat above the pan. Place chops on grill rack directly over drip pan. Cover and grill for 25 to 30 minutes or until juices run clear, brushing chops frequently with glaze during the last 5 minutes of grilling.

To broil: Place the pork chops on the unheated rack of a broiler pan. Broil with surface of chops 3 to 4 inches from heat for 10 to 13 minutes or until juices run clear, turning once and brushing frequently with glaze during last 5 minutes of broiling.

Pork Know-How

Though beef is sold by official (or at least official-sounding) cuts, pork has evolved in the marketplace into six preferred forms. (1) Chops can be boneless or bone-in, thick or thin, and they can come from the center loin, sirloin, rib, or top loin. (2) Ribs are ribs, but not simplistically. They can be cut back, spare, or country-style to star in any barbecued dinner. (3) Cutlets are thin, boneless slices from the loin, leg, shoulder, or tenderloin. (4) Roasts are larger cuts from the same places, perfect for roasting in the oven or using indirect heat on your grill. The two additional pork cuts are (5) strips (a stir-fry favorite) and (6) cubes (just right for kabobs or traditional stews).

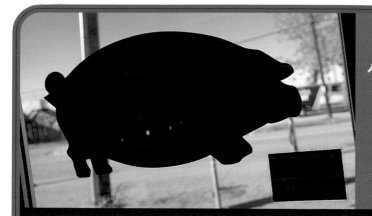

The satés of Indonesia (meat, chicken, or seafood grilled on wooden skewers) usually pair up with a peanut sauce. That special sauce finds a mate with these chops (no skewers required, but authentic Southeast Asian flavor nonetheless).

Pork Chops with
Spicy Peanut Sauce

Prep Time: 15 minutes
Cooking Time: 10 minutes

⅓	cup canned coconut milk
¼	cup creamy peanut butter
¼	cup chicken broth
2	tablespoons canned diced green chili peppers
1	tablespoon diced pimiento
1	tablespoon reduced-sodium soy sauce
2	cloves garlic, minced
1	teaspoon sugar
½	teaspoon ground ginger
½	teaspoon ground coriander
4	boneless pork loin chops, cut ¾ inch thick
	Salt and pepper
1	tablespoon cooking oil
	Green onion slivers (optional)

For sauce, in a small saucepan heat the coconut milk until almost boiling; remove from heat. Stir in the peanut butter, chicken broth, chili peppers, pimiento, soy sauce, garlic, sugar, ginger, and coriander. Cook and stir over medium heat until thickened and smooth.

Sprinkle the pork chops with salt and pepper. In a large skillet cook chops in hot oil for 10 to 12 minutes or until juices run clear, turning once. If desired, top with green onion slivers. Serve chops with the sauce. Makes 4 servings.

Almost everybody is fond of pork with applesauce, but the applesauce is usually a side dish. This recipe includes a sauce of fresh apples, brown sugar, and cream. This sauce not only complements the chops, but it garners center stage.

Apple Sauced
Chops

Total Prep and Broiling Time: 30 minutes

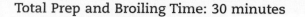

- 1 teaspoon ground cinnamon
- ½ teaspoon dried thyme, crushed
- ¼ teaspoon onion salt
- ¼ teaspoon dry mustard
- 4 pork loin chops, cut 1¼ inches thick (about 2¼ pounds total)
- 2 tablespoons margarine or butter
- 1 medium onion, cut into thin wedges
- 1 large cooking apple (such as Rome Beauty), cored and thinly sliced
- 1 tablespoon brown sugar
- ½ cup whipping cream

For spice rub, in a small bowl stir together the cinnamon, thyme, onion salt, and dry mustard.

Trim fat from the pork chops. Sprinkle spice rub evenly over chops; rub in. Place pork chops on the unheated rack of a broiler pan. Broil with surface of chops 3 to 4 inches from the heat for 18 to 22 minutes or until juices run clear, turning once.

Meanwhile, for sauce, in a medium skillet heat margarine or butter over medium-low heat until melted. Add the onion. Cover and cook for 13 to 15 minutes or until onion is tender. Uncover; add apple slices and brown sugar. Cook and stir over medium-high heat about 5 minutes or until onions are golden and apples

are tender. Carefully stir in the whipping cream. Bring just to boiling; reduce heat. Boil gently for 2 to 3 minutes or until sauce is slightly thickened. Serve sauce over chops. Makes 4 servings.

To grill directly: Grill the chops on the grill rack of an uncovered grill directly over medium coals for 25 to 35 minutes or until the juices run clear, turning once. Serve as above.

To grill indirectly: In a grill with a cover arrange preheated coals around drip pan. Test for medium heat above the pan. Place chops on grill rack directly over drip pan. Cover and grill for 35 to 40 minutes or until juices run clear. Serve as above.

Pork Chops with Chipotle Honey Barbecue Sauce

Prep Time: 30 minutes
Baking Time: 25 minutes
Marinating Time: 6 to 24 hours
Grilling Time: 30 minutes

1   pound plum tomatoes
    Nonstick spray coating
¼   cup canned chipotle peppers in adobo sauce, drained (about ¼ of a 7-ounce can)
2   tablespoons snipped fresh oregano
1   tablespoon Roasted Garlic or bottled minced roasted garlic
¾   cup honey
¼   cup molasses
¼   cup cider vinegar
1   tablespoon toasted sesame oil
1½ teaspoons ground cumin
1   teaspoon salt
6   boneless pork loin chops, cut 1¼ inches thick

Core and halve the tomatoes; scoop out seeds. Spray the unheated rack of a broiler pan with nonstick coating. Place tomato halves on rack, cut sides down. Broil with surface of tomatoes 3 to 4 inches from the heat for 4 to 5 minutes or until skins are charred. Cool until easy to handle. Peel off and discard skins.

Place the undrained chipotle peppers with adobo sauce in a food processor bowl or blender container. Cover and process or blend until smooth. Add the tomatoes, oregano, and Roasted Garlic. Cover and process or blend until smooth. Transfer to a mixing bowl. Stir in the honey, molasses, vinegar, sesame oil, cumin, and salt. (If desired, the mixture may be prepared up to 3 days ahead; cover and refrigerate.)

Trim fat from the pork chops. Place chops in a plastic bag set in a shallow dish. Reserve 1 cup of the tomato mixture; cover and refrigerate. Pour remaining tomato mixture over chops. Close bag. Marinate chops in the refrigerator for at least 6 hours or up to 24 hours, turning the bag occasionally.

Drain the chops, discarding marinade. In a grill with a cover arrange preheated coals around a drip pan. Test for medium heat above the pan. Place pork chops on grill rack directly over the drip pan. Cover and grill for 30 to 35 minutes or until juices run clear.

Meanwhile, in a small saucepan heat the reserved tomato mixture until hot. Spoon hot tomato mixture onto 6 dinner plates. Top tomato mixture on each plate with a grilled chop. Makes 6 servings.

Roasted Garlic: For garlic, peel away the dry outer layers of skin from 1 garlic bulb. Leave skins of cloves intact. Cut off the pointed top portion (about ¼ inch) with a knife, leaving the bulb intact but exposing the individual cloves. Place the garlic bulb, cut side up, in a small casserole or baking dish. Brush sides and top of bulb with ½ teaspoon olive oil. Bake garlic, covered, in a 400° oven for 25 to 35 minutes or until cloves feel soft when pressed. When cool enough to handle, press garlic paste from individual cloves. Makes about 2 tablespoons paste.

The Cadillac Ranch restaurant, which overlooks Denver's historic Larimer Square, created this fresh-tasting roasted tomato sauce for pork chops, but the chef reports equal success using it with beef or chicken. A southwestern flavor is added by the chipotles in adobo sauce, which can be found at most supermarkets.

Simplicity in some things is best. This glaze is one such thing. Based on an ingredient as simple as orange juice, it packs a burst of flavor with very little effort. Count on it next time you need a simple dinner that will please finicky eaters. To give the glaze the freshest, brightest accent, use just-squeezed orange juice.

Orange Glazed
Pork Chops

Prep Time: 15 minutes
Broiling Time: 8 minutes

1   tablespoon brown sugar
1   teaspoon cornstarch
½   teaspoon finely shredded orange peel
½   teaspoon grated fresh gingerroot
⅛   teaspoon ground red pepper
½   cup orange juice
1   tablespoon soy sauce
4   pork loin chops, cut ¾ inch thick
     (about 1½ pounds total)

For glaze, in a saucepan combine brown sugar, cornstarch, orange peel, gingerroot, and red pepper. Stir in the orange juice and soy sauce. Cook and stir until bubbly. Cook and stir for 2 minutes more.

Trim fat from the pork chops. Place chops on the unheated rack of a broiler pan. Broil with surface of chops 3 to 4 inches from the heat for 8 to 10 minutes or until the juices run clear, turning once. Brush the chops with the glaze during the last 5 minutes of broiling. Pass remaining glaze. Makes 4 servings.

Pepper Chops
with Maple Butter

Prep Time: 25 minutes
Grilling Time: 35 minutes

- ¼ cup margarine or butter, softened
- 1 tablespoon maple syrup or maple-flavored syrup
- ½ teaspoon finely shredded orange peel
- ⅛ teaspoon ground nutmeg
- 1 teaspoon coarsely ground black pepper
- ¼ teaspoon salt
- 4 pork loin chops, cut 1¼ inches thick (about 2¼ pounds)
- ¼ cup orange juice

For maple butter, in a small mixing bowl beat together the margarine or butter, maple syrup or maple-flavored syrup, orange peel, and nutmeg. Cover and refrigerate until serving time.

In a small mixing bowl stir together the pepper and salt. Trim fat from the pork chops. Generously brush both sides of pork chops with some of the orange juice. Sprinkle the pepper mixture evenly over both sides of chops; rub mixture onto chops.

In a grill with a cover arrange preheated coals around a drip pan. Test for medium heat above the pan. Place pork chops on grill rack directly over drip pan. Cover and grill for 35 to 40 minutes or until juices run clear, brushing with any remaining orange juice during the last 5 minutes of grilling.

Serve pork chops with a spoonful of the maple butter. Makes 4 servings.

To broil: Prepare the maple butter and chops as directed above, except instead of grilling place pork chops on the unheated rack of a broiler pan. Broil with surface of the chops 3 to 4 inches from the heat for 18 to 22 minutes or until juices run clear, turning once. Brush with any remaining orange juice during the last 5 minutes of broiling. Serve as above.

The Sicilian-inspired muffuletta, a New Orleans masterpiece, is a gargantuan sandwich consisting of various meats and cheeses served on a large round loaf of Italian bread and topped with an olive relish. Creative thinking steals the idea of the relish, which finds a place atop these pork chops.

New Orleans
Pork Chops

Total Prep and Cooking Time: 25 minutes

- 4 pork rib or loin chops,
    cut 1 inch thick (about 2 pounds)
- 2 teaspoons cracked black pepper
- 2 cloves garlic, minced
- 1 tablespoon olive oil
- 1 16-ounce jar pickled mixed vegetables (1½ cups)
- ¼ cup chopped pimiento-stuffed green olives
- 1 tablespoon olive oil

Trim fat from the pork chops. In a small mixing bowl stir together the pepper and garlic. Press the mixture evenly onto both sides of the pork chops.

In a large skillet heat 1 tablespoon olive oil over medium heat. Add the pork chops. Cook, uncovered, for 15 to 17 minutes or until juices run clear, turning once.

Meanwhile, for the relish, drain pickled mixed vegetables, reserving 2 tablespoons liquid. Chop vegetables. In a medium mixing bowl stir together the chopped vegetables, olives, reserved liquid, and 1 tablespoon olive oil. Serve chops with the relish. Makes 4 servings.

French bistros inspired this recipe. The combination of top-quality lamb chops with a quickly made sauce of tomato paste, wine, and herbes de Provence is phenomenal comfort food with sophistication.

Bistro Lamb
Chops

Total Time: 25 minutes

8   lamb rib or loin chops, cut ¾ inch thick
    Pepper
2   tablespoons olive oil
    Salt
1   teaspoon tomato paste
2   cloves garlic, minced
¼   cup dry white wine or chicken broth
¼   cup chicken broth
½   teaspoon herbes de Provence, crushed

Trim fat from the lamb chops; sprinkle with pepper. Heat the olive oil in a large skillet over medium-high heat. Add the lamb chops and cook about 3 minutes or until brown. Turn chops; sprinkle with salt. Cook for 2 minutes more. Cover the skillet; reduce heat to low. Cook the lamb chops for 3 to 5 minutes more or until desired doneness.

Remove the lamb chops from the skillet; keep warm. Stir the tomato paste and garlic into the drippings in the skillet. Carefully add the wine, chicken broth, and herbes de Provence. Increase heat to medium-high; simmer about 3 minutes or until the sauce is reduced by about half, stirring frequently. Spoon off fat. Pour the sauce over the lamb chops and serve immediately. Makes 4 servings.

Lovin' That Lamb

If you haven't tried lamb in many years, the lamb sold today may surprise you. There was a time when lamb tasted strong in flavor. Years ago sheep were bred to produce both wool and meat. Today, younger sheep, or lambs, are raised just for eating. Therefore, the meat is lean, tasty, and tender. There are, however, flavor and size differences between imported and domestic lamb. Domestic lamb is often milder in flavor than imported lamb because the animals are grain-fed rather than grass-fed. Lamb cuts from domestic animals are meatier and up to twice the size of the same cuts from imported animals. Domestic lambs are bigger and meatier because of differences in genetics and breeding techniques. ═══

The Chicago Chop House, located "where the city that works eats," sticks to basics with these veal chops. The sauce, a simple combination of wine, broth, and cream, gets a pleasant bite from cracked pepper.

Sautéed Veal
Chops with Peppercorn Sauce

Prep Time: 25 minutes
Baking Time: 10 minutes

- 4   8-ounce veal chops
- 2   tablespoons all-purpose flour
- 2   teaspoons cracked black pepper
- 2   tablespoons cooking oil
- ⅔   cup dry red wine
- ⅔   cup beef broth
- ½   cup whipping cream
- ½   teaspoon salt

Trim fat from the veal chops. Sprinkle the flour on both sides of chops. Press cracked pepper onto tops of veal chops. In a large, heavy oven-going skillet heat oil over medium heat; add chops and cook for 10 minutes, turning once. Remove chops from skillet. Remove skillet from heat.

For sauce, carefully stir wine and beef broth into drippings in skillet. Return skillet to the heat; scrape up any browned bits. Stir in whipping cream and salt. Bring to boiling; reduce heat. Simmer, uncovered, for 10 minutes or until slightly thickened. Return the chops to the skillet. Bake, uncovered, in a 400° oven for 10 minutes or until juices run clear.

To serve, place chops on 4 dinner plates. Spoon sauce over chops. Season to taste with salt. Makes 4 servings.

LEMON-BASIL STEAKS

Prep Time: 15 minutes
Smoking Time: 45 minutes

Sometimes food calls for simplicity rather than drama. If you're longing for the basics, count on pecan, oak, or hickory smoke to simply nudge the great combination of lemon and basil into being even better.

6   to 8 wood chunks or 2 cups wood chips
     (hickory, pecan, or oak)
1½ teaspoons lemon-pepper seasoning
2   teaspoons country-style Dijon-style mustard
2   teaspoons balsamic vinegar
1   teaspoon dried basil, crushed
2   cloves garlic, minced
4   beef ribeye steaks, cut 1 inch thick

At least 1 hour before smoke-cooking, soak wood chunks (for smoker method) or wood chips (for grill method) in enough water to cover. Drain.

For glaze, in a bowl stir together lemon-pepper seasoning, mustard, vinegar, basil, garlic, and ⅛ teaspoon salt. Brush glaze onto both sides of steaks.

Smoker method: In a smoker arrange preheated coals, drained wood chunks, and the water pan according to manufacturer's directions. Pour water into pan. Place steaks on grill rack over pan. Cover and grill. (Allow 45 to 60 minutes for medium-rare to medium doneness.)

Grill method: In a grill with a cover arrange preheated coals around a drip pan. Test for medium heat above pan. Sprinkle half of the chips over coals. Place steaks on grill rack directly over drip pan. Cover and grill. (Allow 16 to 20 minutes for medium-rare or 20 to 24 minutes for medium.) Add remaining chips halfway through grilling. Makes 4 servings.

Chapter 4

Smoked

RUBBED SIRLOIN
with Horseradish Sauce

Once the fare of old England's chop houses, beef and horseradish still pair beautifully. Give your guests the royal treatment with smoked (or grilled) sirloin and a side of creamy horseradish sauce.

Prep Time: 15 minutes
Chilling Time: 1 to 4 hour
Smoking Time: 2 hours

1	2- to 2½-pound beef sirloin steak, cut 1½ inches thick
4	cloves garlic, minced
¾	teaspoon ground cumin
½	teaspoon cracked black pepper
6	to 9 wood chunks or 3 cups wood chips (oak or hickory)
⅓	cup dairy sour cream
2	tablespoons Dijon-style mustard
1	tablespoon snipped fresh chives
2	teaspoons prepared horseradish
¼	cup whipping cream, whipped

Trim fat from steak. In a bowl stir together garlic, cumin, black pepper, and ¼ teaspoon salt. Sprinkle over one side of steak; rub in. Cover; refrigerate 1 to 4 hours.

At least 1 hour before smoke-cooking, soak wood chunks (for the smoker method) or wood chips (for the grill method) in enough water to cover.

Smoker method: Drain the wood chunks. In a smoker arrange preheated coals, drained wood chunks, and the water pan according to manufacturer's directions. Pour water into the pan. Place the steak, seasoned side up, on the grill rack over the water pan. Cover and grill steak to desired doneness. (Allow about 2 hours for medium-rare doneness or about 2½ hours for medium doneness.)

Grill method: Drain wood chips. In a grill with a cover arrange preheated coals around a drip pan. Test for medium heat above pan. Sprinkle half of the drained chips over the coals. Place steak, seasoned side up, on the grill rack directly over the drip pan. Cover and grill steak to desired doneness. (Allow 20 to 22 minutes for medium-rare doneness or 22 to 26 minutes for medium doneness.) Add more wood chips every 15 minutes.

Meanwhile, for sauce, stir together the sour cream, mustard, chives, and horseradish. Fold in the whipped cream. To serve, thinly slice steak across the grain. Pass sauce. Makes 6 servings.

STAY AWAKE STEAK

Prep Time: 10 minutes
Marinating Time: 2 to 24 hours
Smoking Time: 45 minutes

1   medium onion, chopped
½   cup bottled steak sauce or hickory-flavored
      barbecue sauce
¼   to ⅓ cup strong brewed espresso or coffee
2   tablespoons Worcestershire sauce
1   boneless beef top sirloin steak, cut 1 inch thick
      (about 1½ pounds total)
4   to 6 wood chunks or 2 cups wood chips
      (hickory, pecan, or oak)
2   12-ounce cans beer or 3 cups water

For marinade, in a small mixing bowl stir together the onion, steak sauce or barbecue sauce, espresso or coffee, and Worcestershire sauce. Place steak in a plastic bag set in a shallow dish. Pour marinade over steak. Close bag. Marinate in the refrigerator for at least 2 hours or up to 24 hours. Drain, discarding marinade.

At least 1 hour before smoking, soak wood chunks (for the smoker method) or wood chips (for the grill method) in the beer or water.

Smoker method: Drain wood chunks. In a smoker arrange preheated coals, drained wood chunks, and water pan according to manufacturer's directions. Pour water into pan. Place steak on grill rack over water pan. Cover; grill to desired doneness. (Allow 45 to 50 minutes for medium-rare to medium doneness.)

Grill method: Drain wood chips. In a grill with a cover arrange preheated coals around a drip pan. Test for medium heat above pan. Sprinkle one-fourth of the chips over coals. Place steak on grill rack directly over pan. Cover; grill to desired doneness. (Allow 16 to 20 minutes for medium-rare or 20 to 24 minutes for medium doneness.) Add more chips every 15 minutes.

To broil: Place the steak on the unheated rack of a broiler pan. Broil with surface of steak 3 to 4 inches from heat to desired doneness, turning once. (Allow 10 to 15 minutes for medium-rare to medium doneness.) Carve steak into slices. Makes 6 servings.

Ah, the old chuck wagon! It's a safe bet that wagon trains made it west without benefit of an espresso machine. But they did often use brewed coffee to whip up an easy, devilishly good marinade for beef. This update is "grounds" for celebration.

SMOKED FAJITAS

Prep Time: 30 minutes
Marinating Time: 6 to 24 hours
Smoking Time: 50 minutes

1	1- to 1¼-pound beef flank steak
1	cup beer
½	cup lime juice
½	cup chopped onion
3	tablespoons cooking oil
2	tablespoons bottled steak sauce
1	tablespoon chili powder
1	teaspoon ground cumin
4	cloves garlic, minced
1	bay leaf
4	to 6 wood chunks or 2 cups wood chips (oak or hickory)
3	red, yellow, and/or green sweet peppers, cut into thin strips
8	7-inch flour or corn tortillas
1	recipe Pico de Gallo

Score steak by making shallow cuts at 1-inch intervals diagonally across steak in a diamond pattern. Place steak in a plastic bag set in a shallow dish.

For marinade, combine beer, lime juice, onion, oil, steak sauce, chili powder, cumin, garlic, and bay leaf. Pour over steak. Close bag. Marinate in the refrigerator for 6 to 24 hours, turning occasionally.

At least 1 hour before smoke-cooking, soak wood chunks (for the smoker method) or wood chips (for the grill method) in enough water to cover.

Tear off a 24x18-inch piece of heavy foil. Fold in half to make a double thickness of foil that measures 12x18 inches. Place pepper strips in center of foil. Bring up two opposite edges of the foil; seal edges with a double fold. Fold remaining ends to enclose vegetables, leaving space for steam to build. Tear off a 42x18-inch piece of heavy foil. Fold in half to make a double thickness of foil that measures 21x18 inches. Place tortillas in center of foil. Bring up two opposite edges of the foil. Fold foil to completely enclose the tortillas. Prepare Pico de Gallo. Cover and refrigerate until serving time.

Smoker method: Drain wood chunks. In a smoker arrange preheated coals, drained wood chunks, and water pan according to manufacturer's directions. Pour water into pan. Drain steak, discarding marinade. Place steak on the grill rack over the pan. Cover; grill steak to desired doneness. (Allow about 50 minutes for medium-rare doneness or about 1 hour for medium doneness.) Add foil packets of vegetables and tortillas to grill rack during the last 30 minutes of smoking time.

Grill method: Drain wood chips. In a grill with a cover arrange preheated coals around a drip pan. Test for medium heat above pan. Sprinkle drained wood chips over the coals. Drain steak, discarding marinade. Place steak and tortilla packet on the grill rack directly over the drip pan. Place pepper packet on the grill rack directly over hot coals. Cover and grill steak to desired doneness. (Allow 15 to 18 minutes for medium-rare doneness or 18 to 22 minutes for medium doneness.)

To serve, thinly slice steak diagonally across the grain. Divide steak and pepper strips among the tortillas. Roll-up and serve with Pico de Gallo. Makes 4 servings.

Pico de Gallo: In a medium mixing bowl gently stir together 2 plum tomatoes, chopped; 2 green onions, sliced; 1 fresh serrano chili pepper, seeded and chopped; ¼ of a medium cucumber, seeded and chopped; 2 tablespoons snipped fresh cilantro; and ⅛ teaspoon salt. Cover and refrigerate for up to 24 hours.

Most fajitas are stuffed with grilled flank or skirt steak. These are no different, really. They have an affinity for all the usual fixin's—sweet peppers, onions, plus a homemade *pico de gallo*. But these fajitas should prove an exciting variation on a popular theme with their smoky flavor.

BEEF TENDERLOIN
WITH LIME-SAGE AIOLI

Prep Time: 35 minutes
Grilling Time: 16 minutes

3	cups mesquite wood chips
1	recipe Red Onion Potato Cakes (see recipe page 93)
1	recipe Lime-Sage Aioli
2	plum tomatoes, finely chopped (about ⅔ cup)
1	tablespoon snipped fresh chives
1	pound beef tenderloin
1	tablespoon chipotle peppers in adobo sauce
1	clove garlic, minced
¼	teaspoon salt
¼	teaspoon ground black pepper
4	cups torn red chard
1	tablespoon olive oil
2	tablespoons malt vinegar

At least 1 hour before smoke-cooking, soak wood chips in enough water to cover.

Prepare, cover, and refrigerate Red Onion Potato Cakes (do not cook at this point). Prepare Lime-Sage Aioli. Cover and refrigerate until needed. Stir together tomatoes and chives. Cover and refrigerate until needed.

Trim fat from meat; cut meat into four 1-inch thick steaks. In a blender container combine chipotle peppers and garlic. Cover; blend until smooth. Stir in salt and black pepper. Spread evenly over one cut side of steaks.

Drain wood chips. In a grill with a cover arrange preheated coals around a drip pan. Test for medium heat above pan. Sprinkle half of the drained chips over the coals. Place tenderloin steaks on the grill rack directly over the drip pan. Cover and grill steaks to desired doneness. (Allow 16 to 20 minutes for medium-rare doneness or 20 to 22 minutes for medium doneness.) Meanwhile, cook Red Onion Potato Cakes; keep warm. In a large skillet quickly cook the red chard in the hot olive oil for 1 to 2 minutes or until just wilted. Toss with the malt vinegar. Serve steaks with potato cakes, red chard, aioli, and the tomato mixture. Serve immediately. Makes 4 main-dish servings.

Lime-Sage Aioli: In a blender container or food processor bowl combine ¼ cup refrigerated or frozen egg product, thawed; 1 tablespoon snipped fresh sage; 2 teaspoons minced garlic; and 1 teaspoon Dijon-style mustard. Cover and blend or process until smooth. With the motor running, add ½ cup olive oil in a thin steady steam. If necessary, stop the blender or processor and scrape down the sides of the container or bowl. Add 1 tablespoon lime juice, ⅛ teaspoon salt, and ⅛ teaspoon ground black pepper. Cover and blend or process until mixture is combined and creamy. Makes about 1 cup.

Oven Method: Place the steaks on a rack in a shallow roasting pan. Roast in a 425° oven for 16 to 18 minutes or to desired doneness.

In a "desert oasis" setting at the Sheraton Hotel & Suites Tucson, the Ranchers Club has taken southwestern flavors in novel directions. This recipe calls for beef tenderloin and a dash of flavor from lime-sage aioli. The old chuck wagons probably never served anything quite this innovative—or quite this memorable.

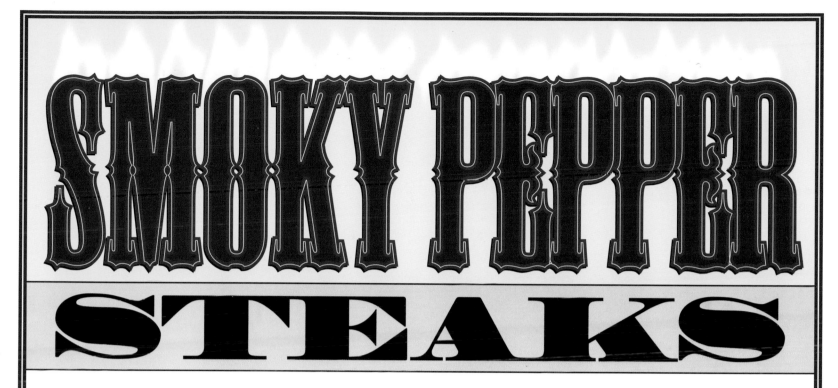

SMOKY PEPPER STEAKS

Prep Time: 15 minutes
Smoking Time: 40 minutes

4 to 6 wood chunks or 3 cups wood chips (pecan, oak, or hickory)
2 to 4 tablespoons finely chopped chipotle peppers in adobo sauce
2 tablespoons lime juice
2 tablespoons cooking oil
4 cloves garlic, minced
¼ teaspoon salt
4 boneless beef top loin steaks, cut 1 inch thick (about 2 pounds total)

At least 1 hour before smoke-cooking, soak wood chunks (for the smoker method) or wood chips (for the grill method) in enough water to cover.

For glaze, in a small mixing bowl stir together the chipotle peppers, lime juice, oil, garlic, and salt. Brush glaze on both sides of steaks.

Smoker method: Drain wood chunks. In a smoker arrange preheated coals, drained wood chunks, and water pan according to manufacturer's directions. Pour water into pan. Place steaks on grill rack over water pan. Cover; grill steaks to desired doneness. (Allow 40 to 60 minutes for medium-rare to medium doneness.)

Grill method: Drain the wood chips. In a grill with a cover arrange preheated coals around a drip pan. Test for medium heat above the drip pan. Sprinkle half of the drained chips over the coals. Place the steaks on the grill rack directly over the drip pan. Cover and grill steaks to desired doneness. (Allow 16 to 20 minutes for medium-rare doneness or 20 to 24 minutes for medium doneness.) Add the remaining chips halfway through grilling.

To broil: Place the steaks on the unheated rack of a broiler pan. Broil with surface of steaks 3 to 4 inches from heat to desired doneness, turning once. (Allow 10 to 12 minutes for medium-rare doneness or 12 to 15 minutes for medium doneness.) Makes 4 servings.

Chipotle peppers in adobo sauce, readily available in Latin markets and in the international aisle at your supermarket, offer a shortcut to giving strip steaks more flair. Just a handful of ingredients is all you need for the sauce. The rest is simply flame and smoke.

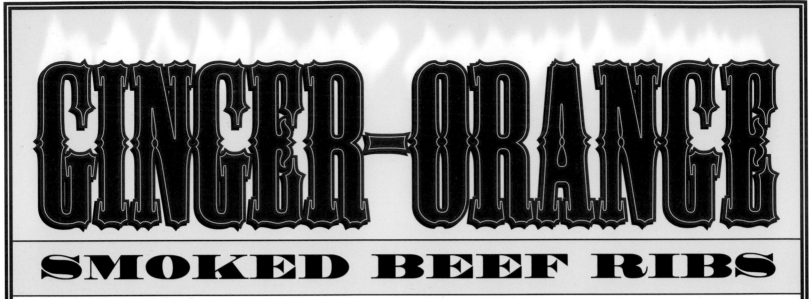

GINGER-ORANGE
SMOKED BEEF RIBS

Prep Time: 10 minutes
Smoking Time: 2½ hours

4   to 6 wood chunks or 3 to 4 cups wood chips
     (oak or hickory)
2   teaspoons paprika
1   teaspoon salt
½   teaspoon pepper
3   to 4 pounds beef back ribs (about 8 ribs)*
½   cup bottled barbecue sauce
¼   cup frozen orange juice concentrate, thawed
2   tablespoons soy sauce
1   tablespoon grated fresh gingerroot

At least 1 hour before smoke-cooking, soak wood chunks (for smoker method) or wood chips (for grill method) in enough water to cover.

For the dry rub, in a small bowl combine the paprika, salt, and pepper. Sprinkle mixture evenly over both sides of ribs; rub mixture onto ribs.

Smoker method: Drain wood chunks. In a smoker arrange preheated coals, drained wood chunks, and water pan according to manufacturer's directions. Pour water into pan. If desired, place ribs in a rib rack. Place ribs on the grill rack over the water pan. Cover and smoke for 2½ to 3 hours or until tender.

Grill method: Drain wood chips. In a grill with a cover arrange preheated coals around a drip pan. Test for medium heat above pan. Sprinkle one-fourth of the chips over the coals. If desired, place ribs in a rib rack. Place ribs on the grill rack directly over the drip pan. Cover; grill for 1¼ to 1½ hours or until tender. Add more wood chips every 20 minutes and more coals as needed.

Meanwhile, for sauce, stir together the barbecue sauce, orange juice concentrate, soy sauce, and gingerroot. Brush ribs with sauce once or twice during the last 15 minutes of smoking or grilling. Pass any remaining sauce. Makes 4 servings.

*Note: Ribs may be purchased in a rack or cut into individual pieces. If left as a rack, cut into individual pieces to serve.

There's the Rub
Cooks are in for a rich area of exploration when they experiment with both marinades and rubs. The two are not the same, of course, but serve a similar purpose: adding more flavor. A marinade is a seasoned liquid that can also tenderize—if it contains an acidic ingredient, such as lemon juice, yogurt, wine, or vinegar. A small amount of oil helps ingredients adhere to the meat better. A rub is a blend of herbs and spices rubbed into the surface of meat. A rub doesn't tenderize. Some cooks prefer rubs made into pastes by adding a little oil, crushed garlic, or mustard.

If you think soy, ginger, and orange are all flavors reserved for Chinese cooking, then you risk missing some great flavor combinations. The orange in particular transforms these ribs to extraordinary cuisine suited to any American table.

BBQ BABY BACK RIBS

Prep Time: 15 minutes
Smoking Time: 3 hours

- 10 to 12 wood chunks or 4 cups wood chips (apple or hickory)
- 2 to 3 slabs meaty pork loin back ribs (about 4 pounds total)
- 2 tablespoons barbecue seasoning
- 1 tablespoon garlic powder
- 1 teaspoon onion salt
- ½ teaspoon celery seed, ground
- ¼ teaspoon ground red pepper
- ½ to ¾ cup bottled barbecue sauce

Nobody wants to start a shootin' war by declaring one city the barbecue capital of America, but certainly Kansas City vies for the title. From nearby Overland Park come these exemplary baby backs, the creation of Boardroom Bar-B-Q. Go ahead, as the folks at Boardroom put it, "Sauce yourself silly."

At least 1 hour before smoke-cooking, soak wood chunks (for the smoker method) or wood chips (for the grill method) in enough water to cover.

Trim fat from ribs. In a small mixing bowl stir together the barbecue seasoning, garlic powder, onion salt, celery seed, and red pepper. Rub the seasoning mixture evenly onto both sides of the ribs.

Smoker method: Drain wood chunks. In a smoker arrange preheated coals, drained wood chunks, and water pan according to manufacturer's directions. Pour water into pan. If desired, place ribs in a rib rack. Place ribs on grill rack over water pan. Cover and grill ribs for 3 to 4 hours or until tender.

Grill method: Drain wood chips. In a grill with a cover arrange preheated coals around a drip pan. Test for medium heat above the pan. Sprinkle one-fourth of the drained chips over the coals. If desired, place ribs in a rib rack. Place the ribs on the grill rack directly over the drip pan. Cover and grill for 1¼ to 1½ hours or until tender. Add more wood chips every 15 minutes and more coals as needed.

Heat the barbecue sauce and pass with the ribs.

Makes 6 to 8 servings.

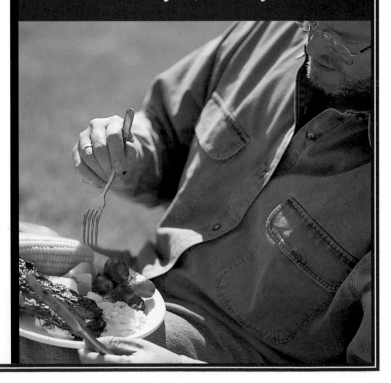

SPICY HOISIN-HONEY RIBS

Prep Time: 30 minutes
Chilling Time: 1 to 4 hours
Smoking Time: 3¾ hours

1 tablespoon paprika
½ teaspoon coarsely ground black pepper
¼ teaspoon onion salt
1 lime, cut in half
4 pounds meaty pork loin back ribs
10 to 12 wood chunks or 4 cups wood chips
   (oak or hickory)
1 to 2 tablespoons finely chopped canned chipotle
   peppers in adobo sauce or 2 dried chipotle peppers
½ cup bottled hoisin sauce
¼ cup honey
2 tablespoons cider vinegar
2 tablespoons Dijon-style mustard
2 cloves garlic, minced

In a bowl combine paprika, black pepper, and onion salt. Squeeze and rub the cut surfaces of the lime halves over ribs. Sprinkle paprika mixture evenly over both sides of ribs; rub in. Cover; refrigerate for 1 to 4 hours.

At least 1 hour before smoke-cooking, soak wood chunks (for the smoker method) or wood chips (for the grill method) in enough water to cover.

Smoker method: Drain wood chunks. In a smoker arrange preheated coals, drained wood chunks, and the water pan according to the manufacturer's directions. Pour water into pan. If desired, place the ribs in a rib rack. Place the ribs on the grill rack over the water pan. Cover and grill the ribs for 3¾ to 4 hours or until tender.

Grill method: Drain wood chips. In a grill with a cover arrange preheated coals around a drip pan. Test for medium heat above the pan. Sprinkle one-fourth of the drained chips over the coals. If desired, place ribs in a rib rack. Place the ribs on the grill rack directly over the drip pan. Cover and grill ribs for 1¼ to 1½ hours or until tender. Add more wood chips every 15 minutes and more coals as needed.

Meanwhile, for sauce, if using dried chipotle peppers, soak them in warm water for 30 minutes; drain well and finely chop. In a small saucepan stir together the hoisin sauce, chipotle peppers, honey, cider vinegar, mustard, and garlic. Cook and stir over low heat until heated through. Just before serving, brush ribs with sauce. Pass remaining sauce. Makes 6 to 8 servings.

The smoky taste of the Southwest comes to these ribs by way of the dried chipotle peppers and from the addition of soaked hardwood to the smoker (or grill) for extra-flavorful smoke. The sauce blends the sweetness of honey and hoisin with the pungence of Dijon mustard.

MUSTARD-BOURBON
GLAZED RIBS

Never underestimate the contribution bourbon can make to a barbecue. In this outing, it joins forces with molasses, brown sugar, and soy for a taste that does its Kentucky heritage proud.

Prep Time: 10 minutes
Chilling Time: 1 to 4 hour
Smoking Time: 3¾ hours

- 1½ teaspoons pepper
- ¾ teaspoon paprika
- ½ teaspoon garlic salt or onion salt
- 3 to 3½ pounds pork country-style ribs
- 10 to 12 wood chunks or 4 cups wood chips (oak or hickory)
- ¼ cup brown mustard
- ¼ cup bourbon or orange juice
- ¼ cup molasses
- 2 tablespoons brown sugar
- 2 tablespoons soy sauce
- 1 teaspoon cooking oil

In a small mixing bowl stir together the pepper, paprika, and garlic or onion salt. Sprinkle the seasoning mixture evenly over both sides of the ribs; rub the mixture onto ribs. Cover and refrigerate the ribs for 1 to 4 hours.

At least 1 hour before smoke-cooking, soak wood chunks (for the smoker method) or wood chips (for the grill method) in enough water to cover.

Smoker method: Drain wood chunks. In a smoker arrange preheated coals, drained wood chunks, and water pan according to manufacturer's directions. Pour water into pan. If desired, place ribs in a rib rack. Place ribs on the grill rack over the water pan. Cover and grill ribs for 3¾ to 4 hours or until tender.

Grill method: Drain wood chips. In a grill with a cover arrange preheated coals around a drip pan. Test for medium heat above pan. Sprinkle one-fourth of the chips over the coals. If desired, place ribs in a rib basket. Place ribs on the grill rack directly over drip pan. Cover and grill for 1½ to 2 hours or until tender. Add more wood chips every 15 minutes and more coals as needed.

Meanwhile for sauce, in a small saucepan stir together the mustard, bourbon or orange juice, molasses, brown sugar, soy sauce, and cooking oil. Cook and stir over low heat until heated through. Just before serving, brush ribs with sauce. Pass remaining sauce. Makes 4 servings.

CHOPS WITH CHERRY SALSA

Prep Time: 20 minutes
Smoking Time: 1¾ hours

½	cup dried cherries, snipped
½	cup bottled chili sauce
½	teaspoon finely shredded orange peel
¼	cup orange juice
2	tablespoons thinly sliced green onion
6	to 9 wood chunks or 3 cups wood chips (cherry or apple)
4	pork loin chops, cut 1½ inches thick (about 2½ pounds total)
	Salt and pepper

For salsa, in a small saucepan combine the cherries, chili sauce, orange peel, orange juice, and green onion. Bring just to boiling; remove from heat. Cool. Serve at room temperature.

At least 1 hour before smoke-cooking, soak wood chunks (for smoker method) or wood chips (for the grill method) in enough water to cover.

Trim fat from the pork chops. Sprinkle both sides of the chops with salt and pepper.

Smoker method: Drain wood chunks. In a smoker arrange preheated coals, drained wood chunks, and water pan according to manufacturer's directions. Pour water into pan. Place chops on the grill rack over the water pan. Cover and grill chops for 1¾ to 2¼ hours or until juices run clear.

Grill method: Drain wood chips. In a grill with a cover arrange preheated coals around a drip pan. Test for medium heat above pan. Sprinkle half of the drained chips over the coals. Place the chops on the grill rack directly over the drip pan. Cover and grill the chops for 35 to 40 minutes or until juices run clear. Add more wood chips every 15 minutes. Serve the chops with salsa. Makes 4 servings.

Salsas, once a trend, are becoming a mainstay of creative cooking. Salsa, the Spanish word for sauce, includes a wide spectrum of tasty, texture-rich chopped toppings that add intrigue to many dishes. Although salsas are often tomato based, this tart-sweet cherry salsa buddies up with chili sauce and orange juice for a unique combo.

CARIBBEAN CHOPS

WITH MANGO SAUCE

Jerk pork is a national dish of Jamaica, a blessed marriage of spice and smoke. Without so much as an air ticket, you can bring legendary Boston Bay near Port Antonio to your own kitchen or grill. For the blue water and white sand, unfortunately, you're on your own.

Prep Time: 20 minutes
Smoking Time: 1½ hours

- 6 to 9 apple or cherry wood chunks or 3 cups apple or cherry wood chips
- 4 pork loin chops, cut 1½ inches thick (about 2½ pounds total)
- 2 to 3 teaspoons Jamaican jerk seasoning
- 1 medium mango, peeled, seeded, and finely chopped (about 1 cup)
- 2 green onions, sliced
- 2 tablespoons snipped fresh parsley or snipped fresh cilantro
- ½ teaspoon finely shredded orange peel
- 2 teaspoons orange juice
- ¼ teaspoon Jamaican jerk seasoning

At least 1 hour before smoke-cooking, soak the wood chunks (for the smoker method) or the wood chips (for the grill method) in enough water to cover.

Trim fat from the pork chops. Rub the 2 to 3 teaspoons jerk seasoning evenly onto both sides of the chops.

Smoker method: Drain wood chunks. In a smoker arrange preheated coals, drained wood chunks, and water pan according to manufacturer's directions. Pour water into pan. Place chops on the grill rack over the water pan. Cover and grill chops for 1½ to 1¾ hours or until juices run clear.

Grill method: Drain wood chips. In a grill with a cover arrange preheated coals around a drip pan. Test for medium heat above pan. Sprinkle half of the drained chips over the coals. Place the chops on the grill rack directly over the drip pan. Cover and grill chops for 35 to 40 minutes or until juices run clear. Add more wood chips every 15 minutes.

Meanwhile, for sauce in a medium mixing bowl stir together mango, green onion, parsley or cilantro, orange peel, orange juice, and ¼ teaspoon Jamaican jerk seasoning. Let stand at room temperature for 15 to 20 minutes. Serve mango sauce over chops. Serves 4.

How Touching

Many home cooks have meat thermometers, but you can judge a steak's doneness just by touch. Experts say rare should feel like the area between your thumb and index finger when that arm is hanging relaxed—soft and spongy. For medium-rare, the same area feels springy but not hard when you form a loose fist. And for medium, the meat will feel similar to that same area when the fist is tightly clinched—firm, with minimal give.

fixin's

grilled sweet potatoes and Apples

Prep Time: 20 minutes
Grilling Time: 20 minutes

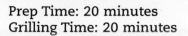

2	medium sweet potatoes, peeled and cut into 1-inch cubes
2	medium cooking apples, cored and cut into eighths
¼	cup maple-flavored syrup
1	teaspoon finely shredded lemon peel
¼	teaspoon ground cinnamon
⅛	teaspoon salt
⅛	teaspoon pepper

In a covered medium saucepan cook sweet potatoes in a small amount of boiling water for 10 minutes. Drain.

Tear off a 36x18-inch piece of heavy foil. Fold foil in half to make a double thickness of foil that measures 18x18 inches. Place the sweet potatoes and apple pieces in center of foil. In a small mixing bowl stir together the syrup, lemon peel, cinnamon, salt, and pepper. Drizzle over apples and potatoes. Bring up 2 opposite edges of foil and seal edges with a double fold. Fold remaining ends to completely enclose the potatoes and apples, leaving space for steam to build.

Grill foil packet on the grill rack of an uncovered grill directly over medium coals for 20 to 25 minutes or until apples are tender. Makes 4 servings.

To cook on rangetop: In a covered medium saucepan cook sweet potatoes in a small amount of boiling water for 10 minutes. Add apple slices. Cook, covered, for 5 to 10 minutes more or until potatoes and apples are tender. Drain. In a small mixing bowl stir together the syrup, lemon peel, cinnamon, salt, and pepper. Drizzle over potatoes and apples. Toss to coat.

YES EVERYTHING'S BIGGER N TEXAS

Though this side dish tastes great anytime, it doubles as a special holiday dish too. When the days shorten and chilly air blasts from the north, autumn flavors like these warm the spirit.

Summer
fruit salad

Prep Time: 25 minutes
Chilling Time: 1 to 6 hours

3 tablespoons frozen orange or
   pineapple juice concentrate, thawed
1 tablespoon honey
2 teaspoons snipped fresh mint or
   ½ teaspoon dried mint, crushed
⅔ cup dairy sour cream
   Lettuce leaves
4 cups mixed fresh fruits (such as blueberries;
   halved strawberries; raspberries;
   peeled, pitted, and sliced peaches;
   peeled, seeded, and chopped mangoes;
   peeled and sliced kiwifruit; cubed honeydew;
   cubed cantaloupe; pitted dark sweet cherries;
   and/or pitted and sliced apricots)

For dressing, stir together the orange or pineapple juice concentrate, honey, and mint. Stir in sour cream.

Cover and chill in the refrigerator for at least 1 hour or up to 6 hours.

To serve, line 6 salad plates with lettuce leaves. Top each with some of the mixed fruit. Stir salad dressing and spoon over the fruit. Makes 6 servings.

Need a summer cooldown? Fresh fruit salad and a lively citrus dressing deliver a refreshing escape from the heat. And if you're the one making the salad, you can fill it with all your favorite summer fruits.

Buttermilk potato salad

Every dedicated griller seeks the perfect potato salad. Maybe it doesn't exist— personal taste being what it is. But if there were a perfect potato salad, it probably would taste a lot like this.

Prep Time: 40 minutes
Chilling Time: 6 to 24 hours

4	medium potatoes (about 1½ pounds)
¼	teaspoon salt
¾	cup mayonnaise or salad dressing
⅓	cup buttermilk
2	tablespoons prepared spicy brown mustard
¼	teaspoon ground black pepper
¼	teaspoon salt
2	cloves garlic, minced
1	cup sliced celery
¾	cup chopped red, orange, or green sweet pepper
4	green onions, sliced
⅓	cup chopped sweet or dill pickles
¼	cup shredded carrot
4	hard-cooked eggs, coarsely chopped
	Lettuce leaves (optional)

Place potatoes in a medium saucepan. Add enough water to cover and ¼ teaspoon salt. Bring to boiling; reduce heat. Simmer, covered, for 20 to 25 minutes or until potatoes are just tender. Drain well. Cool slightly. Peel and cube potatoes.

For dressing, in a large mixing bowl stir together the mayonnaise or salad dressing, buttermilk, mustard, black pepper, ¼ teaspoon salt, and the garlic. Stir in the celery, sweet pepper, green onions, chopped pickles, and carrot. Add the potatoes and eggs. Toss lightly to coat. Cover and refrigerate for 6 hours or up to 24 hours.

To serve, if desired, spoon salad into a lettuce-lined salad bowl. Makes 8 servings.

Red Onion potata cakes

Prep Time: 45 minutes
Cooking Time: 4 minutes (per batch)

- 6 medium potatoes (about 2 pounds)
- ⅓ cup finely chopped red onion
- 2 teaspoons olive oil or cooking oil
- ½ teaspoon salt
- ¼ teaspoon pepper
- 2 tablespoons olive oil or cooking oil

Wash and scrub potatoes with a soft vegetable brush. Cut into quarters. Place quarters in a steamer basket over boiling water. Cover and steam for 15 to 20 minutes or until tender. Remove from steamer. Let stand until cool enough to handle. Peel potatoes. Place in a large bowl. Mash with a potato masher. (Or, peel and quarter the potatoes. Cook in a large covered saucepan with a small amount of boiling, lightly salted water for 20 to 25 minutes or until tender. Drain. Mash with a potato masher or beat with an electric mixer on low speed.)

Meanwhile, cook onion in the 2 teaspoons hot oil until tender. Add to potatoes along with salt and pepper. Shape mixture into 8 patties, about 3 inches in diameter. Place on baking sheet. (If desired, cover and refrigerate until ready to cook.)

In a large skillet cook potato cakes, four at a time, in the 2 tablespoons hot olive oil over medium heat for 4 to 6 minutes or until golden brown, carefully turning once. (If necessary, add additional oil during cooking.) Remove from skillet and keep warm. Repeat with remaining patties. Serve with Beef Tenderloin with Lime-Sage Aioli (recipe on page 78). Makes 8 patties.

The Ranchers Club of Arizona prides itself in serving "copious portions" of meat grilled over four kinds of wood. These potato cakes, topped off with smoked Beef Tenderloin and Lime-Sage Aioli (see recipe page 78), is one of the specialties of the house.

Blue Cheese stuffed potatoes

Prep Time: 15 minutes
Baking Time: 1½ hours

4	large baking potatoes (about 8 ounces each)
½	cup dairy sour cream
¼	cup crumbled blue cheese (1 ounce)
1	tablespoon snipped fresh chives or thinly sliced green onion tops
1	tablespoon snipped fresh parsley
¼	teaspoon garlic salt
⅛	teaspoon pepper
	Milk (optional)

Wash and scrub potatoes thoroughly with a brush; pat dry. Prick potatoes with a fork. Bake in a 350° oven for 70 to 80 minutes or until tender. Cut a lengthwise slice from the top of each potato. Discard skin from slice and place pulp in a bowl. Scoop pulp out of each potato, leaving a ¼-inch-thick shell. Add pulp to the bowl.

Mash the potato pulp with a potato masher or an electric mixer on low speed. Add the sour cream, blue cheese, chives or green onion tops, parsley, garlic salt, and pepper. Stir or beat until smooth. (If necessary, stir in 1 to 2 tablespoons milk to make mixture of desired consistency.) If desired, season to taste with additional garlic salt and pepper. Spoon the potato mixture into the potato shells. Place in a 2-quart rectangular or square baking dish.*

Bake potatoes, uncovered, in a 425° oven about 20 minutes or until lightly browned. Makes 4 servings.

Grill method: Place potatoes in a disposable foil pan. In a grill with a cover place the pan on the grill rack directly over medium-hot coals. Cover and grill for 20 to 25 minutes or until the potatoes are heated through and lightly browned.

*Note: You can prepare the potatoes up to 24 hours ahead up to this point. Cover and refrigerate the potatoes. To heat, bake chilled potatoes, uncovered, in a 425° oven for 25 to 30 minutes or until lightly browned and potatoes are heated through.

It's the age of stuffed potatoes—they've even invaded the fast-food kingdom of French fries. But, as with most things, homemade often tastes better. And if you love blue cheese, these spuds are definitely for you.

greek pasta Salad

Prep Time: 35 minutes
Chilling Time: 2 to 24 hours

6	ounces packaged dried mostaccioli (about 2 cups)
4	plum tomatoes, chopped
½	of a medium cucumber, halved lengthwise and sliced
2	green onions, sliced
3	tablespoons sliced pitted ripe olives
¼	cup olive oil or salad oil
¼	cup lemon juice
1	tablespoon anchovy paste (optional)
1	tablespoon snipped fresh basil or
	1 teaspoon dried basil, crushed
1	tablespoon snipped fresh oregano or
	1 teaspoon dried oregano, crushed
3	cloves garlic, minced
⅛	teaspoon salt
⅛	teaspoon pepper
½	cup crumbled feta cheese (2 ounces)

In a large saucepan cook the mostaccioli in a large amount of boiling salted water about 14 minutes or until the pasta is al dente. Drain. Rinse with cold water. Drain.
In a large mixing bowl toss together the cooked mostaccioli, tomatoes, cucumber, green onions, and olives. In a screw-top jar combine the olive oil or salad oil, lemon juice, anchovy paste (if using), basil, oregano, garlic, salt, and pepper. Cover and shake well. Drizzle over pasta mixture. Toss to coat. Cover and chill in the refrigerator for at least 2 hours or up to 24 hours. Add feta cheese. Toss before serving. Makes 6 to 8 servings.

The fresh herbs, oils, and olives that characterize Greek cuisine complement mostaccioli in this sprightly pasta salad. Top this dish with a flourish of feta cheese crumbles. Any grilled steak you serve it with will be smitten.

Garlic Mashed
Colorado potatoes

Happily, garlic has become one of the favored seasonings in everyday cooking. When something so simple can add so much great flavor, why not incorporate a bulb or two into foods? Here's a winning rendition of mashed potatoes from the Buckhorn Exchange in Denver that does just that with smashing results.

Total Time: 30 minutes

3	pounds Colorado red potatoes or other red potatoes
⅔	cup butter
¼	cup finely chopped garlic
1	teaspoon dried minced garlic (optional)
⅔	cup freshly grated Parmesan cheese
1	teaspoon salt
¼	teaspoon pepper
⅔	to 1 cup half-and-half or light cream, warmed

Wash the potatoes and scrub thoroughly with a vegetable brush. Cut potatoes in halves or quarters. In a large Dutch oven combine potatoes and enough cold water to cover. Bring to boiling; reduce heat. Simmer, uncovered, for 15 to 20 minutes or until tender.

Meanwhile, in a small saucepan combine the butter, chopped garlic, and dried minced garlic, if using. Cook, stirring occasionally, over very low heat until the butter bubbles. Remove from heat. Keep warm.

Drain potatoes. Place in a large mixing bowl. Add the Parmesan cheese, salt, and pepper. Mash potatoes with a potato masher or beat with an electric mixer on low speed. Stir in the garlic mixture until combined.

Gradually beat in the half-and-half or light cream until mixture is light and fluffy. Makes 10 servings.

2-Cheese
potato casserole

Prep Time: 20 to 35 minutes
Chilling Time: 4 to 24 hours
Baking Time: 45 minutes

6	medium potatoes (2 pounds)
½	cup dairy sour cream
½	teaspoon salt
3	to 4 tablespoons milk
2	ounces smoked cheddar cheese or cheddar cheese, shredded
2	ounces Monterey Jack cheese with jalapeño peppers or Monterey Jack cheese, shredded

Grease a 1½-quart casserole. Set aside. Peel potatoes. Quarter potatoes. In a covered large saucepan cook potatoes in boiling salted water for 20 to 25 minutes or until tender. Drain.

Mash the drained potatoes with a potato masher or beat with an electric mixer on low speed. Add the sour cream and salt. Gradually beat in enough milk to make smooth and fluffy. Gently stir in the shredded cheeses. Spoon into prepared casserole. Bake immediately or cover and refrigerate for at least 4 hours or up to 24 hours.

To serve, bake casserole, uncovered, in a 350° oven for 45 to 50 minutes or until heated through. Makes 6 servings.

This hearty side dish truly is Americana all the way. It's easy to make and passes as prime comfort food (even for people who thought they were comfortable enough already).

Chocolate-Walnut BROWNIE PUDDING

A brownie better than your mother's—is it possible? This one actually can be traced back to the '40s, so maybe it is your grandmother's. We don't want to start a generational squabble over a brownie but this one is better than average. The rich bittersweet chocolate sauce under the brownie's surface begs for a scoop of ice cream.

Prep Time: 15 minutes
Baking Time: 40 minutes
Standing Time: 45 minutes

1	cup all-purpose flour
¾	cup granulated sugar
2	tablespoons unsweetened cocoa powder
2	teaspoons baking powder
¼	teaspoon salt
½	cup milk
2	tablespoons cooking oil
1	teaspoon vanilla
½	cup chopped walnuts
¾	cup packed brown sugar
¼	cup unsweetened cocoa powder
1½	cups boiling water

Grease an 8x8x2-inch baking pan. Set aside.

In a medium mixing bowl stir together the flour, granulated sugar, the 2 tablespoons cocoa powder, the baking powder, and salt. Stir in the milk, oil, and vanilla. Stir in the walnuts.

Pour into the prepared pan. In a small mixing bowl stir together the brown sugar and the ¼ cup cocoa powder. Stir in the boiling water; slowly pour over batter in pan. Bake in a 350° oven for 40 minutes. Cool in pan on a wire rack for 45 to 60 minutes. Serve warm. If desired, serve with ice cream. Makes 6 to 8 servings.

Chapter 6

desserts

Famous Dave's
BREAD PUDDING

This simple edition of popular bread pudding deserves to be as famous as Dave Anderson of Minneapolis who created it. Although most well-known for his good-and-messy barbecue creations, Dave also makes a mean bread pudding. Look for Dave (perhaps taste-testing his bread pudding) at locations of his Famous Dave's BBQ Shacks.

Prep Time: 15 minutes
Baking Time: 1 hour

½	cup golden raisins
8	cups cubed challah or other egg bread (8 ounces)
5	beaten eggs
3	cups milk
1	cup whipping cream
¾	cup sugar
1	tablespoon vanilla
½	teaspoon ground cinnamon
	Vanilla ice cream
	Bottled praline or caramel sauce

Grease a 9x9x2-inch baking pan. Sprinkle the raisins in the prepared pan. Layer the challah over raisins. In a large mixing bowl stir together the eggs, milk, whipping cream, sugar, vanilla, and cinnamon. Pour over bread and raisins, pushing down any visible pieces of bread.

Bake in a 325° oven about 1 hour or until a knife inserted near center comes out clean. Cool slightly. Serve warm with ice cream and sauce. Makes 8 servings.

Country Pear and CHERRY CRISP

In the past few years, America has enjoyed the rediscovery of a whole repertoire of wonderful homemade sweets. Even the novice cook will triumph with this fruity crisp.

Prep Time: 15 minutes
Baking Time: 30 minutes

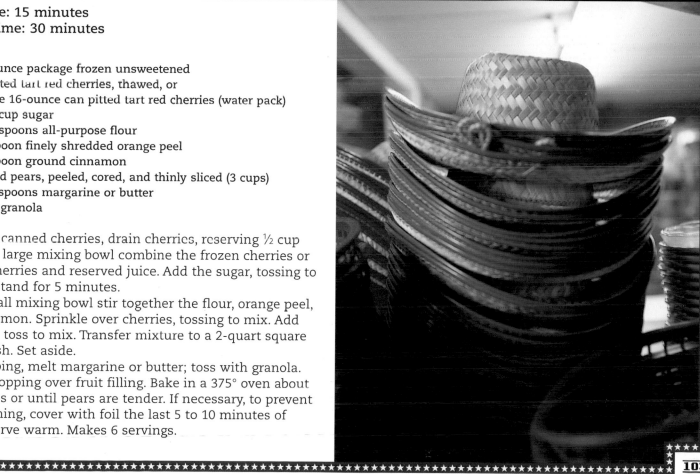

- 1   16-ounce package frozen unsweetened pitted tart red cherries, thawed, or one 16-ounce can pitted tart red cherries (water pack)
- ⅓   to ½ cup sugar
- 2   tablespoons all-purpose flour
- 1   teaspoon finely shredded orange peel
- ½   teaspoon ground cinnamon
- 1   pound pears, peeled, cored, and thinly sliced (3 cups)
- 2   tablespoons margarine or butter
- 1½ cups granola

If using canned cherries, drain cherries, reserving ½ cup juice. In a large mixing bowl combine the frozen cherries or canned cherries and reserved juice. Add the sugar, tossing to coat. Let stand for 5 minutes.

In a small mixing bowl stir together the flour, orange peel, and cinnamon. Sprinkle over cherries, tossing to mix. Add the pears; toss to mix. Transfer mixture to a 2-quart square baking dish. Set aside.

For topping, melt margarine or butter; toss with granola. Sprinkle topping over fruit filling. Bake in a 375° oven about 30 minutes or until pears are tender. If necessary, to prevent overbrowning, cover with foil the last 5 to 10 minutes of baking. Serve warm. Makes 6 servings.

Corn Bread CHERRY COBBLER

If you've lost track of how your mother or grandmother used to make this no-fail crowd-pleaser, here's a terrific way out of the woods. Choose from either the corn bread topper or the traditional topper.

Prep Time: 30 minutes
Baking Time: 12 minutes

4	cups pitted tart red cherries or one 16-ounce package frozen unsweetened pitted tart red cherries
⅔	cup sugar
2	tablespoons cornstarch
2	tablespoons orange juice
⅓	cup cornmeal
3	tablespoons all-purpose flour
1	tablespoon sugar
1	tablespoon finely chopped pecans
¾	teaspoon baking powder
2	tablespoons butter
1	slightly beaten egg white
1	tablespoon milk
1½	teaspoons granulated sugar
⅛	teaspoon ground cinnamon
	Half-and-half or light cream or vanilla ice cream (optional)

For filling, in a medium saucepan combine the cherries, the ⅔ cup sugar, the cornstarch, and orange juice. Let fresh cherries stand for 10 minutes or let frozen cherries stand for 20 minutes. Cook and stir mixture over medium heat until thickened and bubbly. Cook and stir 1 minute more. Reduce heat and keep hot.

Meanwhile, for biscuit topping, in a medium mixing bowl stir together the cornmeal, flour, the 1 tablespoon sugar, the pecans, and baking powder. Cut in the butter until the mixture resembles coarse crumbs.

In a small mixing bowl combine the egg white and milk. Add all at once to the flour mixture, stirring just until moistened. Spoon the hot fruit mixture into a 1½-quart casserole. Immediately spoon the biscuit topping into 4 or 8 mounds over the hot fruit mixture. Stir together the 1½ teaspoons sugar and the cinnamon. Sprinkle sugar mixture over the biscuit mounds.

Bake cobbler in a 400° oven for 12 to 15 minutes or until a wooden toothpick inserted into the center of a biscuit mound comes out clean. If desired, serve cobbler warm with half-and-half, light cream, or ice cream. Makes 4 servings.

Graham Cherry Cobbler: Prepare the Corn Bread Cherry Cobbler as above, except for the topping omit the cornmeal and the 1 tablespoon sugar. Increase the flour to ⅓ cup, add 2 tablespoons finely crushed graham crackers, and 1 tablespoon brown sugar. Increase the milk to 2 tablespoons. Continue as above.

Rhubarb-Pineapple CRUMBLE

Any way you crumble it, this fruit dessert will make any cowboy (or cowgirl) take notice. A crumble consists of fruit that is topped with a crumbly, sweetened pastry mixture then baked until bubbly hot. A treat like this one naturally deserves a scoop or two of vanilla ice cream (try Brown Sugar-Vanilla Ice Cream on page 113).

Prep Time: 30 minutes
Standing Time: 1 hour
Baking Time: 1 hour

7   cups fresh or frozen rhubarb,
        cut into 1-inch pieces
1   8-ounce can crushed pineapple, drained
1   cup packed brown sugar
2   tablespoons cornstarch
2   teaspoons finely shredded lemon peel
⅔   cup all-purpose flour
¼   cup packed brown sugar
1   tablespoon granulated sugar
1   tablespoon chopped crystallized ginger
        Dash salt
⅓   cup butter
        Vanilla ice cream (optional)

If using frozen rhubarb, thaw completely; drain well. In a large mixing bowl combine the fresh or thawed rhubarb, pineapple, and the 1 cup brown sugar. Let stand 1 hour. Drain mixture, reserving juices. If necessary, add water to reserved juices to measure ⅔ cup liquid.

Place the juices in a small saucepan. Stir in the cornstarch. Cook and stir over medium heat until thickened and bubbly. Remove saucepan from heat. Stir the cornstarch mixture into the rhubarb mixture; stir in the lemon peel. Transfer the mixture to a 2-quart square baking dish.

In a medium mixing bowl stir together the flour, the ¼ cup brown sugar, the granulated sugar, ginger, and salt. Using a pastry blender, cut in the butter until mixture is crumbly. Spoon over fruit. Bake in a 350° oven about 1 hour or until light brown and bubbly. If desired, serve warm with ice cream. Makes 6 to 8 servings.

Banana
STREUSEL PIE

Banana pie sheds the traditional whipped cream for an old-fashioned streusel topper. The nuts contribute a satisfying contrast of crunch to the smooth filling.

Prep Time: 35 minutes
Baking Time: 40 minutes

1   recipe Pastry for Single-Crust Pie
4   cups sliced bananas (about 5)
½   cup unsweetened pineapple juice
2   tablespoons lemon juice
1½ teaspoons finely shredded lemon peel
¼   cup granulated sugar
½   teaspoon ground cinnamon
1   teaspoon cornstarch
½   cup all-purpose flour
½   cup packed brown sugar
⅓   cup chopped macadamia nuts or almonds
1   teaspoon ground cinnamon
¼   cup butter

Prepare and roll out Pastry for Single-Crust Pie. To transfer pastry, wrap it around the rolling pin; unroll into a 9-inch pie plate. Ease pastry into pie plate, being careful not to stretch pastry. Line the unpricked pastry shell with a double thickness of foil. Bake in a 450° oven for 8 minutes. Remove foil. Bake 4 to 6 minutes more or until pastry is golden. Remove from oven. Reduce oven temperature to 375°.

Meanwhile, in a bowl gently toss together the bananas, pineapple juice, and lemon juice. Drain, reserving juices. Gently toss bananas with the lemon peel, granulated sugar, and the ½ teaspoon cinnamon. Spoon mixture into pastry shell. In a saucepan combine the reserved juices and the cornstarch. Cook and stir over medium heat until thickened and bubbly. Pour over banana mixture in shell.

For streusel, combine the flour, brown sugar, nuts or almonds, and the 1 teaspoon cinnamon. With a pastry blender or 2 forks, cut in the butter until mixture resembles coarse crumbs. Sprinkle over banana mixture. Cover the edge of pie with foil. Bake in a 375° oven for 40 minutes or until topping is golden brown and edge is bubbly. Cool on wire rack. Makes 8 servings.

Pastry for Single-Crust Pie: Stir together 1¼ cups all-purpose flour and ¼ teaspoon salt. Using a pastry blender, cut in ⅓ cup shortening until pieces are pea-size. Sprinkle 1 tablespoon cold water over part of the mixture; gently toss with a fork. Push moistened dough to side of bowl. Repeat, using 4 to 5 tablespoons water total, until all the dough is moistened. Form dough into a ball. On a lightly floured surface, flatten dough ball. Roll from center to edge into a circle about 12 inches in diameter. Continue as directed.

APPLE PIE
with Cider Sauce

Prep Time: 30 minutes
Baking Time: 50 minutes

1   recipe Pastry for Double-Crust Pie
⅔   to ¾ cup sugar
1   tablespoon all-purpose flour
½   teaspoon ground cinnamon
⅛   teaspoon ground nutmeg
6   cups thinly sliced, peeled apples
1   cup dried mixed fruit bits, raisins, or dried cherries
2   tablespoons milk
2   teaspoons sugar
   Ice cream (optional)
   Cider Sauce (optional)

Prepare and roll out Pastry for Double-Crust Pie. Line a 9-inch pie plate with half of the pastry. To transfer the pastry, wrap it around the rolling pin; unroll it into a 9-inch pie plate. Ease the pastry into the pie plate, being careful not to stretch pastry. In a large mixing bowl stir together the ⅔ to ¾ cup sugar, the flour, cinnamon, and nutmeg. Add the apple slices; gently toss until coated. Sprinkle dried fruit evenly over bottom of the pastry-lined pie plate. Top with apple mixture. Trim pastry to edge of pie plate. Roll remaining pastry to a circle about 12 inches in diameter. Cut slits in pastry circle; place on filling and seal. Crimp edge as desired.

Brush the top crust with the milk. Sprinkle with the 2 teaspoons sugar. To prevent overbrowning, cover edge of pie with foil. Bake pie in a 375° oven for 25 minutes. Remove foil. Bake for 25 to 30 minutes more or until top is golden. (Prepare Cider Sauce, if using, while pie bakes.) Cool pie on a wire rack. If desired, serve with ice cream and/or warm Cider Sauce. Makes 8 servings.

Pastry for Double-Crust Pie: Stir together 2 cups all-purpose flour and ½ teaspoon salt. Using a pastry blender, cut in ⅔ cup shortening until pieces are pea-size. Sprinkle 1 tablespoon cold water over part of the mixture; gently toss with a fork. Push moistened dough to side of bowl. Repeat, using 6 to 7 tablespoons water total, until all the dough is moistened. Divide dough in half. Form each half into a ball. On a lightly floured surface, flatten 1 dough ball. Roll from center to edge into a circle about 12 inches in diameter.

Cider Sauce: In a medium saucepan combine 2 cups apple cider or apple juice and 6 inches stick cinnamon. Bring to boiling; reduce heat. Simmer, uncovered, about 20 minutes or until liquid is reduced to 1 cup. Strain through a sieve or colander lined with 100% cotton cheesecloth. Discard cinnamon. In the saucepan melt 3 tablespoons margarine or butter; stir in 2 tablespoons honey and 1 tablespoon cornstarch. Stir in the cider mixture. Cook and stir until thickened and bubbly. Cook and stir for 2 minutes more. Serve warm.

A common fate for apples is to become pie or cider. Here the two work together in this intriguing recipe. Whether you prefer open-faced apple pie or double-crusted delight, the cider sauce, kissed with cinnamon then enriched with butter and honey, will set your rendition apart.

BROWNIES

Prep Time: 20 minutes
Baking Time: 30 minutes

- 1 cup sugar
- ½ cup butter
- ⅓ cup unsweetened cocoa powder
- 2 eggs
- 1 teaspoon vanilla
- ⅔ cup all-purpose flour
- ½ teaspoon baking powder
- ¼ teaspoon salt
- ½ cup chopped walnuts
- 1 recipe Cocoa Glaze

Grease an 8x8x2-inch baking pan. Set aside.
In a medium saucepan combine the sugar, butter, and cocoa powder. Cook and stir over medium heat until butter melts. Remove from heat; cool for 5 minutes. Add the eggs and vanilla. Using a spoon, beat lightly just until combined. Stir in the flour, baking powder, and salt. Stir in the walnuts. Spread batter into the prepared pan. Bake in a 350° oven for 30 minutes. Cool on a wire rack. Frost with Cocoa Glaze. Makes 16 servings.

Cocoa Glaze: In a medium mixing bowl stir together 1 cup sifted powdered sugar and 2 tablespoons unsweetened cocoa powder. Beat in 2 tablespoons softened margarine or butter and ¼ teaspoon vanilla with an electric mixer on low to medium speed. Beat in enough boiling water (1 to 2 tablespoons) to make a smooth glaze.

When you crave an old-fashioned brownie, here's the recipe of choice. Nothing really out of the ordinary—just simple bites of chocolate pleasure to share after a good steak dinner.

Black Walnut SPICE CAKE

It's hard to pass up wonderful black walnut spice cake. But the maple-cream cheese frosting is the best part about this recipe. You'll most likely get requests for seconds. If you're partial to regular walnuts (English walnuts), you can substitute them for the black walnuts, which have a distinctive, strong flavor.

Prep Time: 20 minutes
Baking Time: 25 minutes

1	cup all-purpose flour
¾	cup sugar
1	teaspoon ground cinnamon
½	teaspoon baking powder
½	teaspoon baking soda
¼	teaspoon ground allspice
⅛	teaspoon salt
½	cup buttermilk or sour milk*
¼	cup margarine or butter, softened
1	egg
¼	teaspoon vanilla
½	cup chopped black walnuts
1	recipe Maple-Cream Cheese Frosting

Grease an 8x8x2-inch baking pan. Set aside.
In a large mixing bowl stir together the flour, sugar, cinnamon, baking powder, baking soda, allspice, and salt. Add the buttermilk or sour milk, butter, egg, and vanilla. Beat with an electric mixer on low speed until combined. Beat on high speed 2 minutes more. Stir in the black walnuts.

Pour batter into the prepared pan. Bake in a 350° oven for 25 to 30 minutes or until a wooden pick inserted near the center comes out clean. Cool cake in pan on a wire rack. Spread with Maple-Cream Cheese Frosting. Cover and store in the refrigerator. Makes 9 to 12 servings.

Maple-Cream Cheese Frosting: In a small mixing bowl beat half of a 3-ounce package softened cream cheese, 2 teaspoons maple-flavored syrup, and ¼ teaspoon vanilla with an electric mixer on low to medium speed until fluffy. Gradually add 1¼ cups sifted powdered sugar, beating well. Beat in enough milk (about 1 to 2 teaspoons) to make the frosting easy to spread.

***Note:** To make ½ cup sour milk, place 1½ teaspoons lemon juice or vinegar in a glass measuring cup. Add enough milk to make ½ cup total liquid; stir. Let the mixture stand for 5 minutes before using it in the recipe.

Mississippi MUD CAKE

"Mississippi Mud" is a moniker for any number of chocolate cakes. The name may sound peculiar—at least until you taste this ultra rich and slightly gooey concoction. Irresistible. So forget what your mom told you about not playing in the mud and dig in!

Prep Time: 20 minutes
Baking Time: 30 minutes

1 cup butter
⅓ cup unsweetened cocoa powder
4 eggs
2 cups sugar
1½ cups all-purpose flour
1 teaspoon vanilla
¼ teaspoon salt
8 ounces miniature marshmallows
  (a scant 5 cups)
1 recipe Creamy Chocolate Frosting

Grease a 13x9x2-inch baking pan. Set aside.
In a medium saucepan combine the butter and cocoa powder; cook and stir over low heat until butter is melted. In a large mixing bowl beat the eggs with an electric mixer on medium speed until well mixed.

Add the sugar, flour, and butter-chocolate mixture; beat well. Add the vanilla and salt; beat well.

Pour batter into the prepared pan. Bake in a 350° oven for 30 to 35 minutes or until a wooden toothpick inserted near the center comes out clean. Sprinkle with the marshmallows; return to the oven for 2 to 3 minutes to melt marshmallows. Remove from the oven; cool in the pan on a wire rack. Spread with the Creamy Chocolate Frosting; cut into bars. Store in an airtight container at room temperature for up to 3 days. Makes 36 servings.

Creamy Chocolate Frosting: In a medium saucepan combine ⅓ cup unsweetened cocoa powder and ¼ cup butter; cook and stir over low heat until the butter is melted. Remove from heat. Gradually beat in 2 cups sifted powdered sugar with an electric mixer on low speed. Beat in 2 tablespoons milk. Gradually beat in another 2 cups sifted powdered sugar and enough milk to make the frosting easy to spread.

Brown Sugar-Vanilla ICE CREAM

When you're making your own ice cream, the listed ingredients are only the beginning. It's your chance to get creative in the kitchen. This recipe, with its variations, gets you started. But for the pure at heart, the basic recipe is a tasty twist on vanilla.

Prep Time: 25 minutes
Freezing Time: 40 minutes
Ripening Time: 4 hours

2	cups half-and-half or light cream
1	cup packed brown sugar
2	beaten egg yolks
3	cups whipping cream
1	tablespoon vanilla
½	cup chopped pecans or almonds, toasted (optional)

In a large saucepan combine the half-and-half or light cream, and brown sugar. Cook and stir over medium heat just until brown sugar dissolves (mixture may appear curdled). Stir about 1 cup of the mixture into the beaten egg yolks; return all to the saucepan. Bring to boiling, stirring constantly; reduce heat. Boil gently over medium-low heat for 2 minutes, stirring constantly.

Stir in the whipping cream and the vanilla. Cool. If desired, stir in the pecans or almonds. Freeze in a 4- or 5-quart ice-cream freezer according to the manufacturer's directions. Ripen ice cream for 4 hours. Makes 8 servings (about 2 quarts).

White Chocolate and Nut Ice Cream: Prepare Brown Sugar-Vanilla Ice Cream as directed, except use ¾ cup granulated sugar instead of the brown sugar and use almonds instead of pecans. In the saucepan combine the half-and-half or light cream with the granulated sugar. Cook as directed at left, except stir 4 ounces of melted white baking bars or ⅔ cup melted white chocolate pieces into the hot, cooked egg mixture, stirring until mixture is smooth (about 3 minutes). Continue as above. If desired, serve ice cream with fresh strawberries, blueberries, or raspberries.

Double Peanut Ice Cream: Prepare Brown Sugar-Vanilla Ice Cream as above, except omit the pecans or almonds. Stir ⅔ cup creamy peanut butter in with the uncooked egg yolks. (Mixture will be thick.) Cook as directed at left. Stir in ½ cup chopped unsalted dry roasted peanuts just before freezing. If desired, serve the ice cream with hot fudge sauce.

Grilled Banana SUNDAES

Finally, a dessert you fix right on the grill after all the steaks, chops, and ribs are done. Even the sauce can be made in a pan over the coals. Three cheers for sundaes and picnics!

Total Prep/Grilling Time: 15 minutes

- 3 large firm bananas
- 1 tablespoon margarine or butter, melted
- 2 teaspoons orange juice
- ½ cup caramel ice-cream topping
- ¼ teaspoon ground cinnamon
- 1 pint vanilla ice cream
  Toasted coconut
  Sliced almonds, toasted

Cut bananas in half lengthwise, then cut each piece in half crosswise. (You should have 12 pieces.) Stir together margarine or butter and 1 teaspoon of the orange juice.

Brush mixture on all sides of the banana pieces. Place the bananas on the grill rack of an uncovered grill directly over medium-hot coals. Grill for 2 minutes; turn bananas over and grill for 2 minutes more or until heated through.

Meanwhile, for the sauce, in a heavy, medium skillet or saucepan combine the caramel topping and the remaining orange juice. Heat the caramel mixture on the grill rack alongside bananas directly over the coals or on a stovetop until the mixture boils, stirring frequently. Stir in the cinnamon. Add the bananas to the sauce and stir gently to coat.

To serve, scoop ice cream into 4 dessert dishes. Spoon sauce and bananas over ice cream. Sprinkle with the coconut and almonds. Makes 4 servings.

Where do I find it?

Metric Cooking Hints

By making a few conversions, cooks in Australia, Canada, and the United Kingdom can use the recipes in *Better Homes and Gardens® Steaks, Ribs, Chops and All the Fixin's That Make 'em Great* with confidence. The charts on this page provide a guide for converting measurements from the U.S. customary system, which is used throughout this book, to the imperial and metric systems. There also is a conversion table for oven temperatures to accommodate the differences in oven calibrations.

Product Differences: Most of the ingredients called for in the recipes in this book are available in English-speaking countries. However, some are known by different names. Here are some common American ingredients and their possible counterparts:
■ Sugar is granulated or castor sugar.
■ Powdered sugar is icing sugar.
■ All-purpose flour is plain household flour or white flour. When self-rising flour is used in place of all-purpose flour in a recipe that calls for leavening, omit the leavening agent (baking soda or baking powder) and salt.
■ Light corn syrup is golden syrup.
■ Cornstarch is cornflour.
■ Baking soda is bicarbonate of soda.
■ Vanilla is vanilla essence.
■ Green, red, or yellow sweet peppers are capsicums.
■ Golden raisins are sultanas.

Volume and Weight: Americans traditionally use cup measures for liquid and solid ingredients. The chart, below, shows the approximate imperial and metric equivalents. If you are accustomed to weighing solid ingredients, the following approximate equivalents will be helpful.
■ 1 cup butter, castor sugar, or rice = 8 ounces = about 250 grams
■ 1 cup flour = 4 ounces = about 125 grams
■ 1 cup icing sugar = 5 ounces = about 150 grams
 Spoon measures are used for smaller amounts of ingredients. Although the size of the tablespoon varies slightly in different countries, for practical purposes and for recipes in this book, a straight substitution is all that's necessary.
 Measurements made using cups or spoons always should be level unless stated otherwise.

Equivalents: U.S. = Australia/U.K.

⅛ teaspoon = 0.5 ml
¼ teaspoon = 1 ml
½ teaspoon = 2 ml
1 teaspoon = 5 ml
1 tablespoon = 1 tablespoon
¼ cup = 2 tablespoons = 2 fluid ounces = 60 ml
⅓ cup = ¼ cup = 3 fluid ounces = 90 ml
½ cup = ⅓ cup = 4 fluid ounces = 120 ml
⅔ cup = ½ cup = 5 fluid ounces = 150 ml
¾ cup = ⅔ cup = 6 fluid ounces = 180 ml
1 cup = ¾ cup = 8 fluid ounces = 240 ml
1¼ cups = 1 cup
2 cups = 1 pint
1 quart = 1 liter
½ inch =1.27 cm
1 inch = 2.54 cm

Baking Pan Sizes

American	Metric
8×1½-inch round baking pan	20×4-cm cake tin
9×1½-inch round baking pan	23×3.5-cm cake tin
11×7×1½-inch baking pan	28×18×4-cm baking tin
13×9×2-inch baking pan	30×20×3-cm baking tin
2-quart rectangular baking dish	30×20×3-cm baking tin
15×10×1-inch baking pan	30×25×2-cm baking tin (Swiss roll tin)
9-inch pie plate	22×4- or 23×4-cm pie plate
7- or 8-inch springform pan	18- or 20-cm springform or loose-bottom cake tin
9×5×3-inch loaf pan	23×13×7-cm or 2-pound narrow loaf tin or pâté tin
1½-quart casserole	1.5-liter casserole
2-quart casserole	2-liter casserole

Oven Temperature Equivalents

Fahrenheit Setting	Celsius Setting*	Gas Setting
300°F	150°C	Gas Mark 2 (slow)
325°F	160°C	Gas Mark 3 (moderately slow)
350°F	180°C	Gas Mark 4 (moderate)
375°F	190°C	Gas Mark 5 (moderately hot)
400°F	200°C	Gas Mark 6 (hot)
425°F	220°C	Gas Mark 7
450°F	230°C	Gas Mark 8 (very hot)
Broil		Grill

*Electric and gas ovens may be calibrated using Celsius. However, for an electric oven, increase the Celsius setting 10 to 20 degrees when cooking above 160°C. For convection or forced-air ovens (gas or electric), lower the temperature setting 10°C when cooking at all heat levels.